HISTORIC
HOOSIER
GYMS

HISTORIC
HOOSIER
GYMS

DISCOVERING
BYGONE
BASKETBALL
LANDMARKS

Kyle Neddenriep

Foreword by Angelo Pizzo,
screenwriter & producer of Hoosiers

THE
History
PRESS

Published by The History Press
Charleston, SC 29403
www.historypress.net

Front cover image by Richard Marheine,
www.marheinephotography.com.

Images are courtesy of the author.

First published 2010
Second printing 2011

ISBN 9781540224200

Library of Congress Cataloging-in-Publication Data
Neddenriep, Kyle.
Historic Hoosier gyms : discovering bygone basketball landmarks / Kyle Neddenriep.
p. cm.

1. Basketball--Indiana--History. 2. Gymnasiums--Indiana--History. 3. Historic buildings--
Indiana. I. Title.
GV885.72.I6N43 2010
796.32309772--dc22
2010039761

Notice: The information in this book is true and complete to the best of our knowledge. It is offered
without guarantee on the part of the author or The History Press. The author and The History
Press disclaim all liability in connection with the use of this book.

FOREWORD

The movie isn't called *Hickory*. It's called *Hoosiers*. It's a celebration—like you'll find in this tour of the Indiana gyms—of a statewide tradition, high school basketball, something that got into our blood and took on the shape of a thing larger than mere game.

There's just nothing as uniquely Indiana as high school basketball. Swing open a Hoosier barn door and you expect to find a hoop inside (there's probably one on that barn door as well). It just makes sense here, perhaps in a way that transcends explanation, and perhaps it's a portion of our makeup that shouldn't be demystified. It's who we are.

If we're not playing it, we're devoted to it, likely to a specific team, and in the era this book revisits, that meant something a little different. There was a time when basically every Indiana community had a high school and a basketball team, though not every community had a structure that could serve as a regulation gym. Of course, in the eyes of a Hoosier, there's no place that can't host a game, even if the dimensions don't allow for regulation. So it made sense to turn whatever structure was most accommodating into the team's gym.

It simply made sense to erect a hoop wherever possible, and the townspeople would arrive and cheer and rally around their team—temporarily free from the burdens of work, the stresses of life, those aspects that become so wonderfully trivial in the warmth of the gym—surrounded by one's friends and neighbors and filled with that aspect of oneself that courses through the system in a mystifying way that feels so natural.

So though the form is different now, Indiana high school basketball still thrives. Maybe we all no longer have our own hometown teams, but we still have basketball in our blood, and that's not going to change.

—Angelo Pizzo

ACKNOWLEDGEMENTS

There's no better way to learn about your surroundings than to hit the road and see them for yourself. From December 2008 to August 2010, that's what I did. With an Indiana state map next to me in the car and towns circled with a blue marker, I went in search of old high school gyms.

Even better than the gyms were the people I met along the way, people who went out of their way, above and beyond, to help me find what I was looking for. They invited me into their offices, their schools, their homes. Those conversations have spawned new friendships that I treasure. Indiana may have lost some of its basketball heritage when these towns lost their schools, but the passion for the sport remains deeply embedded in Hoosier culture.

I can't count how many times I got lost along the way. How do you get lost in Bedford? Or nearly run out of gas on a gravel road in rural Crawford County? There were some funny moments, too: the bird that nearly flew directly into my face as I descended the steps of the Kingman gym and a chance meeting with colleague Tom Davis, who lives in the Chili gym. (Unbeknownst to me, I showed up on his front porch one Friday morning in June.)

A special mention goes to the following individuals: Bob Adams, who helped me get started on this project back in 2008. Adams has written his own books about Indiana high school basketball and has extensively researched the history of individual schools. His help was greatly appreciated and necessary. Harley Sheets, who invited me into his home in Danville in the early stages of this project and helped me identify a number of schools to research. Tony Potts, of Washington, who set up a meeting with several former Washington Hatchets and proceeded to lead me to two other gyms in this book. Former newspaperman and author Wendell Trogdon, who

ACKNOWLEDGEMENTS

provided valuable guidance during lunch one day in Mooresville. Bill May, whose book, *Tourney Time*, is a tremendous resource for anyone researching Indiana high school basketball. Bill's knowledge and passion for the game are unmatched. Chris May, the executive director of the Indiana Basketball Hall of Fame. Chris was quick to help in tracking down several of the people quoted in this book. John Ockomon, who has probably visited every one of the gyms in this book. We'll soon review our list of "favorite" gyms, I'm sure. Jim Hartman, of Sullivan, who provided background materials on the Sullivan County gyms. Kristen Leigh Porter, my former boss at the *Indianapolis Star*, who encouraged me to pursue this idea. Brittain Phillips and Joe Gartrell of The History Press, who believed it could be done and provided support and feedback. Ted Green of the *Indianapolis Star*, who helped develop the old gyms idea originally as a print story and online database. Kevin Messmer, of Jasper, who provided photos and background information. Angelo Pizzo, writer and producer of *Hoosiers*, for providing some details about the movie that I'd never heard before. His timeless movie resonates in many of these communities. Bob Whalen, who has extensively researched Crawfordsville basketball history. And Bill Boone, for his photos and background of Ladoga and other Montgomery County gyms.

Also, thanks to the many librarians I bugged for information, particularly those in Mitchell, Jeffersonville, Hebron, Crawfordsville, Camden, Otwell, Versailles and Mt. St. Francis.

And a huge thank you to *Indianapolis Star* photo researcher Dawn Mitchell. Dawn contributed so much of the behind-the-scenes work that made this project possible. There's no way it would have happened without her help. I owe you one.

To my sons, Kyson (three) and Jace (one). Kyson would ask why I was going to look at old gyms and not new ones. My job for you two is to travel these roads together fifty years from now and see how many of these gyms are still around.

And, most important of all, to my wife, Jennifer, who supported me throughout this project. How she manages to hold it all together is beyond me. I love you. (Kind of funny that we actually met in a gym in 1997.)

There's no way to mention everybody who made this book possible, but I thank all of you.

8

INTRODUCTION

We were about halfway through an hour-long interview in April 2010 when John Helm scanned the other faces in the conference room at the Baymont Inn in Washington, Indiana, and then locked in on mine. Something was obviously bugging him.

"I'm not sure how you're going to do this," he said. "You can't describe what it was like back then."

It's true. That era of basketball is behind us. There's no way of going back in time and peeking through the window of a regional game at Bedford's "Quarry," squeezing into an aisle seat at the Church Street Gym in New Castle or climbing a ladder to claim a spot on a wood plank for a game in Economy.

But isn't it fun to imagine?

This book focuses on one hundred former high school basketball gyms in Indiana from a time when virtually every community in the state had its own school. There were a few parameters for inclusion in this book: the gym had to have been used at one time as a high school gym; it could no longer be used as a high school gym; it had to still be standing; and I had to be able to get inside to get a photo.

Sadly, many gyms have been torn down, and little by little, Indiana loses bits of its rich and treasured basketball history. The School Corporation Reorganization Act of 1959 resulted in sweeping consolidation of school districts across the state, and in the ensuing years the gyms—the hub of activity in most Indiana communities—went dark on Friday nights in the winter.

But look hard enough and you can still find these old gyms, remnants of a bygone and uniquely Hoosier era. They were home to the Ladoga Canners and Mecca Arabs, the Oolitic Bearcats and Greens Fork Demons. Now they are elementary schools, community centers, fire stations, private businesses, churches, libraries and even homes.

INTRODUCTION

The stories they could tell! Built mostly from the 1920s to '50s, before the antiseptic, multipurpose athletic facilities of today, each had its own unique feature, such as the crow's-nest scorer's table in Bloomfield, the out-of-bounds walls in Mecca (it wasn't long enough for end lines) and the wraparound balcony in Harrisburg.

This isn't a complete history of every former high school gym in the state. Though the numbers dwindle year by year, there are more than one hundred out there, many in towns that are just a speck on the state map. Through interviews with hundreds of people who played, coached, officiated or remember these gyms as fans, this book is intended to offer a glimpse into what made them unique, the teams that played there and their current uses.

Maybe Helm is right. Maybe you can't describe what it was like to sit on the roof of a small southern Indiana gym and watch through a window as all-black Crispus Attucks played a game in 1948, sit in the front row at the dedication in Sullivan's gym in 1928 or yell from the balcony of the Washington gym in the 1940s.

But you can imagine.

LOCATIONS OF FEATURED GYMS

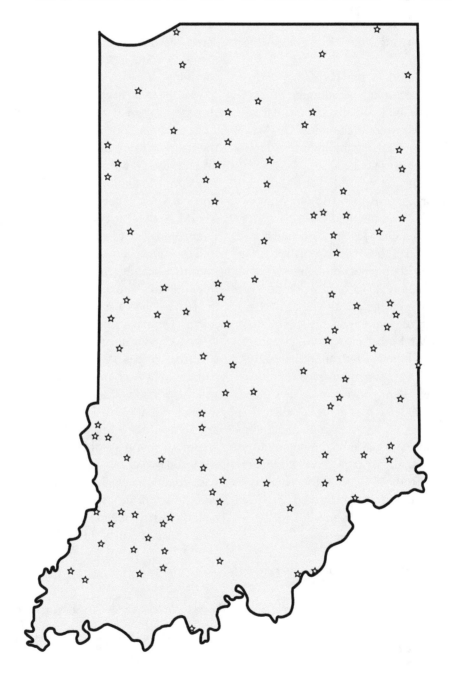

PERU

Brian Strong's curiosity got the best of him.

Newly hired as the Peru High School athletic director in the summer of 2009, Strong dropped off his son at daycare, located in classrooms adjoining Tig-Arena, Peru's vintage 1940 gymnasium. After one look, Strong was hooked.

"I couldn't believe it," he said. "I thought right away that we had to do everything we could to get a game here."

On December 4, 2009, for the first time since the end of the 1990 season, the old Tig-Arena was hopping again. Before a sellout crowd of more than twenty-five hundred fans, Peru defeated rival Wabash 81–35. Among those in attendance were 1975 Indiana Mr. Basketball Kyle Macy and six-foot-eleven John Garrett, an Indiana all-star from 1971 who went on to play at Purdue.

Though Peru moved to a new home for the 1990–91 season (also called Tig-Arena), the old arena remained standing as an important piece of the community's rich basketball heritage. Peru hosted the sectional from 1941 to 1963, winning it seventeen times. It also hosted the 1943 regional, defeating Monticello 36–34 for the regional championship.

"Tig-Arena was a basketball mecca," said Bob Biddle, who coached at Peru for seven seasons beginning in 1958. "It was a true basketball arena, not a bad seat in the house. It was packed for every game. It was hot and it was loud. It was a true showplace, a great venue for basketball."

The Miami Nation of Indians bought the building from the school for $1 in 1990 and has used it for a variety of community functions, including bingo nights three times a week. When Strong approached Miami Nation of Indians vice-chief John Dunnagan about bringing basketball back to Tig-Arena, he was all for it. Dunnagan said the heating bill can run $6,000 a month in the winter.

"Just having [a game here] is the main thing," Dunnagan said. "There's still a use for it. Too many nights it just sits here empty."

Strong hopes the success of the first game at Tig-Arena in almost twenty years will help make the gym a part—albeit a smaller part—of Peru's future. There are many others in the Miami County community who feel the same way.

"It takes you back to the days when basketball was really the only source of entertainment in town," Biddle said. "I've already heard some people ask, 'Why don't we go back and play there all the time?'"

Opposite, top: Tig-Arena, built in Peru in 1940, has been owned by the Miami Nation of Indians since 1990.

Opposite, bottom: An interior look at Tig-Arena in Peru. The team played a "throwback" game in the gym in 2009 to a sellout crowd.

LEBANON

Sometimes the outdoor courts just wouldn't do.

On sweltering summer nights in 1965, just before his senior year, Rick Mount would stop by coach Jim Rosenstihl's house and ask for the key. Usually, it was the coach's wife, Patricia Ann, who answered the door. She knew the key Mount was after was to Lebanon Memory Hall, which filled its twenty-two-hundred-seat capacity throughout Mount's illustrious high school career.

But on these nights, it was just Mount and the basketball echoing as it bounced in the empty gym. The lights from Memory Hall shined out from the high windows into the neighborhood. That caused a problem.

"I'd be in there for a couple hours and lose track of time," said Mount, who still lives in Lebanon. "I didn't realize it, but that light would shine right out into those people's houses. So they called the mayor and complained; he called coach Rosenstihl, and he told me to quit shooting so late at night."

Mount begged his way back into the gym, only after promising to shoot by the light of the moon and the exit sign. In February 1966, Mount would become the first high school athlete to appear on the cover of *Sports Illustrated*. He led Lebanon to a regional championship as a senior and finished his career with 2,595 points, now fourth on the state's all-time list.

"The fans would be right up there close," Mount said of the gym, which was built in 1931. "It was always so hot. Even in the middle of January, they'd open those big windows to cool it off in there."

Lebanon's high school team moved out after the 1967–68 season. Mount took a tour of the new gym while on a break from Purdue.

"Coach Rosenstihl asked me to test out the new baskets," Mount remembered. "He wanted me to make the first shot in the new gym."

The city bought Memory Hall and the adjoining school in 1974, after a new middle school was completed. Though it appeared in a scene in the 1986 movie *Hoosiers*, there was talk of tearing it down in the 1980s and '90s, as it sat empty.

In 1996, Leo Stenz, owner of Stenz Construction Development Corporation in Indianapolis, bought and refurbished the gym and school, turning it into a health club and senior living center.

Memory Hall looks much like it did during Mount's playing days. A portrait of Mount, Indiana's 1966 Mr. Basketball adorns the gym's south end.

"It was a great old gym," said Mount, whose father, Pete, was a star on Lebanon's 1943 state runner-up team. "I'm so glad they didn't tear it down. If it could talk, you wonder what stories it could tell."

This mural where the stage was once located depicts Lebanon's school through the years and honors former Lebanon and Purdue star Rick Mount.

Leo Stentz of Indianapolis bought the Lebanon gym and former school in 1996 and converted it into a health center.

Memory Hall in Lebanon was built in 1931 and was the site of several sectional tournaments.

SANDUSKY

For two years, Chris and Michele Komora searched the United States, looking for an old school to renovate and call home.

"We wanted to find a building that wasn't too huge and unmanageable but something that was unique that we could fix up and keep us busy," said Chris Komora, a Chicago native who is retired from the military. "Also, we are foster-care certified, so the idea of having this much room—and a gym—was really appealing."

In 2003, after looking at more than two hundred schools from Idaho to New York, they found their nirvana: the former Sandusky High School, a few miles north of Greensburg in Decatur County. For

The Sandusky gym was built in 1936. A group of Sandusky alums helped Chris and Michele Komora renovate the school and gym, which they use as their home.

$95,000, the Komoras bought a building that hadn't been used in thirty-five years, with a gym built in 1936 as a Works Progress Administration project.

Rooms were filled with trash. There were dead rodents. The roof leaked. Windows were broken.

As the Komoras worked to restore the building over the next three years, they drew curious stares from residents of the unincorporated town, many of whom were Sandusky graduates.

Some were skeptical, but not all. A group of Sandusky alumni, led by Jim Spillman (class of 1944), helped the Komoras renovate. A new roof was put on the gym, handicapped-accessible bathrooms were added and the bleachers and original goals were scraped and painted.

Now the gym is just another room—a big one—in the house. Named for Spillman, who died in 2007, the gym looks much as it did in 1936. The Komoras hosted a Sandusky reunion in the gym in 2006, twenty-eight years after the previous one.

"I'm thrilled to see it still standing," said Arthur Cleland, a 1947 graduate who helped with the renovation. "Every time we drive past it, it means a lot to see it there. Every game back then would be standing-room only."

KEWANNA

A sign greets visitors coming from the north on Indiana 17 just outside of Kewanna. It proclaims the Fulton County community of six hundred to be "The Little Town With a Big Heart." It's a motto not without merit. For years, much longer than most communities its size, Kewanna fought off the school consolidation that had ripped the pulse of many small towns in Indiana.

The final graduating class of 16 students passed through Kewanna's doors in 1982.

"It was a pretty bustling little town at one time," said Tom Troutman, a 1966 graduate. "They fought off consolidation as long as they could. But like most little towns, it eventually happened."

Depending on their address, Kewanna's students were sent to one of three schools: Caston, Rochester or Winamac. The 1917 school was torn down a few years later, but the gym—built in 1928—was purchased by the Winamac Coil Spring Company in 1985, a family-owned business that moved from Winamac to Kewanna in 1958.

"We purchased it to keep it from becoming a sore sight," said Gene Huber, one of the owners. "We use the classrooms up above the gym for storage and tore out the floor and use the gym part of it for production."

Though it's filled with machinery now, it's not hard to imagine what it looked like as a basketball court. The shell of the stage is still visible on the east end (though the actual stage has been torn out), and there is a balcony on the west end above the cafeteria where elementary and junior high students would congregate during games.

The Kewanna gym, built in 1928, is now used by the Winamac Coil Spring Company. It was so small that Kewanna rarely played its home games there by the 1950s.

The gym had bleachers on just one side—the south—and seated maybe 250 at capacity. By the 1950s, the Indians played many "home" games at neighboring schools, mainly Aubeenaubee Township.

"We'd play a couple home games a year, but the gym was so small," Troutman said. "We had two ten-second lines, which was usually confusing for the other team. It was a great home-court advantage."

Kewanna won sectionals in 1927 (when it played in a basement gym at the old school) and in 1954, but it usually ran up against bigger schools in Rochester or Logansport. The teams in 1965 and '66 combined to go 33-10, led by six-foot-two Ron McColley and five-foot-eleven Jim Talbott. Also a star pitcher on Kewanna's baseball teams, Talbott scored 1,029 points in his career.

On August 6, 1969, just two weeks after his twenty-first birthday, Talbott was killed in combat in Vietnam. The community built a Veterans of Foreign Wars post three years later and named it for Talbott.

"After all these years, we still grieve for him," said Shirley Willard, a former teacher at Kewanna.

SHARPSVILLE

Virginia Chambers took a seat in the first-row bleachers at the O.H. Hughes Memorial Gymnasium—named after the school's first superintendent—just a few feet from where she sat fifty years earlier as a vocal member of the cheer block known as the Bulldog Barkers (complete with a live bulldog).

"It holds a lot of memories," said the former Virginia Henderson, looking out onto the court. "This is what kids did. Friday night, you were here."

Built at a cost of $15,000 in 1926, the Sharpsville gym is all that's left to remind visitors that the rural Tipton County community once had a school of its own. Sharpsville absorbed Prairie Township in 1963–64 and was known as the Sharpsville-Prairie Spartans until 1970, when the school consolidated with Windfall and became known as Tri-Central, located just outside Sharpsville.

The adjoining school building—which was rebuilt after a fire destroyed the original school on February 4, 1928—was used as an elementary school until 1982. It was razed six years later, and a park was erected in its place with money raised by the Sharpsville Park Committee and through a grant from the Tipton County Foundation.

After moving out of its original gym, which was located above a hardware store, the Bulldogs had immediate success, winning the 1927 Tipton Sectional and Anderson Regional. Led by coach Dwight V. Singer, the Bulldogs lost 29–22 to Muncie Central in the first round of the sixteen-team state finals played at the Indianapolis Exposition Center. Sharpsville would go on to claim sectional titles in 1928 and 1948.

The seven-hundred-seat-capacity gym is still used today for league games, reunions, parties and community celebrations, even one wedding. Among its unique features are long vertical windows on the north end and a stage on the south end.

"It was always packed," said Rick Grimme, a 1969 graduate. "A lot of guys, including my dad, would stand up against the wall surrounding the court. They never sat down. We thought it was fun to sit on the stage (on the south end) to catch the ball if came flying up there."

Opposite, top: The Sharpsville gym in Tipton County was built in 1926.

Opposite, bottom: Before playing in this gym, the Sharpsville Bulldogs played in a gym above a hardware store.

MATTHEWS

The unusually wide main street of Matthews recalls a time of great ambition. Located in the center of the Trenton gas field, the Grant County community was a boomtown in the late 1800s, with a population upwards of 100,000 residents and nearly twenty surrounding "suburbs."

Around that time, in the 1890s, a long wood structure called the French Club was built a block east of downtown as one of the growing community's original bar and dance halls. The building was moved to Main Street a few years later, in 1900, and soon found an alternate use as a tiny high school gymnasium.

Doyte Kibbey, interviewed in January 2010 at age ninety-five, is one of the few remaining members of the former Matthews Minutemen. Kibbey graduated from Matthews in 1933, and the school was consolidated with Upland to create Jefferson Township in 1934.

"The story goes that they were named the Minutemen because they were scoring a point a minute," Kibbey said. "That was quite a bit in those days."

Matthews never won a sectional tournament in its short history, but it did advance to the Grant County Tournament championship in 1932, losing by one point to Van Buren. Kibbey was the team captain as a senior. He played "back guard" and rarely crossed half court.

In one home game against nearby Harrison Township in 1933, Kibbey was told by coach Herbert Groninger to smother sharpshooter Jimmy Yeager. He did, holding Yeager to one point. The *Muncie Star* lauded the Minutemen for doing a better job on Yeager than eventual regional champion Muncie Central.

"We had some great games there," Kibbey said. "There wasn't much room, just maybe two rows of spectators and some up on the stage. When the people sat on the bleachers, their feet would be on the playing floor. We had a lot of good teams there over the years and a lot of enthusiasm."

The elementary school students used the facility for many years, into the 1970s, after high school was consolidated. The Lions Club now leases the gym from the town corporation (through the school corporation) for $1 a year, and the building was extensively renovated in 1997, including new metal siding, a new roof and other upgrades for an estimated $15,000.

The gym is available to rent, although it doesn't attract as many visitors as it once did. Kibbey, who lives two blocks from the gym, is one of the few who remember it as a high school gym.

"We feel like it's a service to the community to keep it going," Kibbey said. "We don't cover our expenses, but hopefully there's still a use for it."

The exterior of the Matthews gym, former home of the Matthews Minutemen.

This gym in Matthews was originally known as the French Club in the early 1900s. The Grant County community only had a high school until 1934. The gym is now available to rent.

PERRY CENTRAL

Want to buy a gym? Bob and Ginny Patterson did, and in 1986 they bought the former Perry Central gym in rural Boone County.

The gym, built in 1939, was in bad shape. The windows were boarded up, and the roof was caving in. It was barely salvageable.

For two years, the Pattersons lived in a motor home parked at center court while they refurbished the west end of the building—where there was a stage that overlooked the court—into a cozy home. They turned the area that was once the gym into storage for their business, Fayette Nursery.

"We get people who come up here all the time and tell us how it used to look," Bob Patterson said. "They get a kick out of it."

Perry Central was mostly composed of farmers' kids from the area surrounding the unincorporated village of Fayette. Classes were tiny. Kent Glendenning was part of a seven-person graduating class in 1953.

"At that time, our gym was as nice as any in Boone County," said Glendenning, who was a standout forward on the Midgets' teams in the early '50s. "You could probably only get two hundred people in there, but people would buy season tickets and fill up both sides."

An exterior look at the Perry Central gym.

In the Pattersons' home, there are two upstairs bedrooms. On the south end, one of the locker rooms has been converted into a kitchen; on the north end, where the other locker room was located, is a bathroom. The original brick walls are exposed in both rooms to add to the nostalgic theme. On the west end of the court, an original basket support still hangs from the wall.

"It's a neat little place," Ginny Patterson said.

Perry Central was absorbed by Lebanon, along with nearby Whitestown, in 1963.

In early 2010, the Pattersons put the building, along with their home, up for sale.

"We're just getting to that age where it's more than we can handle," Ginny Patterson said. "But it'd be a great little bachelor pad for someone. It means so much to so many people, hopefully someone can keep it going."

Want to buy a gym?

Ginny Patterson sits at a desk on what was the stage at the Perry Central gym in rural Boone County.

A backboard hangs inside the Perry Central gym.

Bob and Ginny Patterson bought the gym in 1986. They used the gym as a warehouse for their nursery business before putting it up for sale in 2010.

ROLL

Driving though blink-or-you-miss-it Roll in Blackford County, it's difficult to imagine that the community had one shining moment of basketball glory.

For a small school like Roll, winning a sectional was everything—the equivalent of Muncie Central or Marion winning a state title. In 1951, with three sophomores in the starting lineup, the Roll Red Rollers won the school's only sectional title.

"I had a wire recording of the game transferred to cassette and still have it," said Jim Dickey, one of the sophomore starters on that '51 team that defeated Montpelier 40–38 to win the Hartford City Sectional. "It's still fun to listen to."

The school was later absorbed by neighboring Montpelier (five miles east) in 1963, and those two schools, along with Hartford City, combined to become Blackford County in 1969.

Roll is now little more than a ghost town on Highway 18. The school building, which once housed grades one through twelve, was demolished in 1977. But the gym, bought by Dickey and neighbor John Glancy for $100 in 1993, is a reminder that Roll has a history.

Though it's rented out on occasion, there's no money to be made. The only satisfaction is knowing that the gym, built in 1938 as part of the Works Progress Administration projects of the 1930s and '40s, is still there.

"When they took the school away, the town died," Dickey said. "That gym is about all that's left."

Dickey admits he doesn't know how much time it has. Though the original floor is still in good condition and the gym can still serve a purpose, there aren't many kids around to use it. The days have long passed since Roll's model steam roller—a large tricycle was concealed underneath—would chug its way around the court during timeouts.

"It's getting a little run-down now," Dickey said. "I worry that it will eventually be like the school, where the roof starts to cave in. It would be a dream come true if somebody came in and saved it. I don't know if anybody will."

Above: The Roll Red Rollers used this as their home gym when they won a sectional in 1951.

Opposite, inset: Roll residents and alums Jim Dickey and John Glancy bought the Roll gym in 1993. It was built in 1938 and is now available to rent, although business has slowed in the tiny Blackford County community.

ARLINGTON

George Sutton squints through the falling snow on a dark January evening and looks into the past. In his eyesight is the old Arlington school, built in 1909 and, until 2010, used by the elementary students of the Rush County community. But a new elementary school has gone up across town, leaving the old school in limbo.

Sutton, eighty, has lived across the street from the school for thirty-six years.

"Yesterday's gone," Sutton said. "It has value, but only in the minds of those of us who remember it. It's like a pumpkin at the end of the vine."

Though its days may be numbered, the Arlington gym is a reminder of Hoosier past. Built in 1939, it features a rounded roof common of gyms built in that era. There is permanent seating raised off the floor—similar to the Knightstown gym—and several rows of bleachers behind the east basket. Producers from the 1986 movie *Hoosiers* toured the gym but ultimately decided not to use it.

The Arlington Purple Breezes had their heyday in the 1940s, winning the Rushville Sectional in 1942 and '47. The school consolidated into Rushville, along with nearly all the other county schools, in 1968.

"We had fun, lots of fun, in that gym and saw a few fights," said Priscilla Winkler, a

Like many of its era, this gym in Arlington was built through the Works Progress Administration (later Work Projects Administration), a relief measure established in 1935 to aid the unemployed.

1955 Arlington graduate. "The fights were usually between the adults, not the kids."

Though the gym remains in pristine condition, its future is uncertain. On one cold, winter night, a light is on in the gym. Looking through an outside window, the door leading to the court is halfway open. The gym is empty, silent. One wonders how it must have bustled on those Friday nights when those Arlington teams of the 1940s played a home game.

"Time goes on," said Sutton, sounding like a man who wanted to believe otherwise.

The Arlington gym was built in 1939 and was the home of the Purple Breezes until consolidation in the late 1960s. It was used by the elementary school until 2010. Its future is uncertain.

MILROY

When a visitor asks to see the old high school gym at Milroy Elementary School, Mike Ralston replies, "Which one? Old or new?"

Ralston, a maintenance worker at the school and a 1958 graduate, has given this tour before. The school, an elementary in the Rush County community until a new school was built in the spring of 2010, is actually the home of two former gyms used by the Milroy Cardinals.

When the school was constructed in 1913, a basement room was designed specifically for a gym. It was considered a luxury at the time, as many high schools played on makeshift courts located above taverns or stores. With a concrete floor, a low ceiling and enough space for maybe one hundred spectators, it hardly seems luxurious by today's standards.

"My dad played in that gym," said Lowell Ennis, whose father, also named Lowell, played on Milroy's 1920 sectional championship team. "They had some good teams. Growing up, I knew all those guys he played with. They were all farm boys, just like we were."

Milroy was one of twelve teams to advance to the state finals in Bloomington in 1920. The Cardinals lost to Hartford City, 34–24, in their first game and finished with a 27-3 record.

By 1928, Milroy had outgrown its basement gym, and the community paid for a modern gym to be built adjacent to the

A new elementary school was scheduled to be ready by the fall of 2010, and it was undetermined what would happen to the old school and gym.

school. With dark wood bleachers on both sides, it seated about seven hundred people.

"It was one of the nicest gyms in the county," said Ennis, eighty-one, a farmer who lives a half mile east of town. "That hardwood court was one of the best around."

Ennis was a junior on the 1946 team that finished 20-4, won the Rushville Sectional and won a regional game over Brownsville. The next year, with Ennis, Joe Woods, Jules Harcourt, Wayne Wilson and Kermit Harcourt in the starting lineup, the Cardinals went 20-3 but lost to rival Arlington in the sectional.

"We had a lot of fun playing the game," Ennis said. "It seems like everyone's out for blood and guts today."

As of the spring of 2010, the fate of the Milroy school was undecided. The "old gym" and the "new gym" could become just memories.

Milroy had one of the best gyms in Rush County when this gym was built in 1928.

This tiny basement gym in Milroy is typical of where teams played before basketball-only gyms were built in the 1920s.

ECONOMY

Hugging the north side of U.S. 35 in the tiny community of Economy (population two hundred), in Wayne County, is a white barn. At least, it looks like a barn. On Wednesday nights, the lights from the white barn shine out of four glass windows, and the clock turns back to the 1940s and '50s, when fans of the Economy Cardinals would pack it for basketball games.

Wednesdays are open gym nights in Economy. Teenagers from the area no longer play for Economy, which consolidated into nearby Hagerstown in 1963. But at least for a couple hours a week, they have a chance to see how it used to be. The gym, built in 1924, features a sixty-one-foot court (twenty-three feet short of a regulation high school floor).

"I'd cry my eyeballs out if they ever tore this place down," said Bud Tutterrow, a 1960 Economy graduate and caretaker of the gym, which is owned by Perry Township. "I'd buy it myself and give it [back] to the township if it ever came to that."

The Economy gym is one of the oldest and most intimate of the former high school gyms still standing in Indiana. The wall on the east end of the gym serves as the out-of-bounds "line." Same of the stage on the west end, which offers a perilous landing spot for players rushing in for a layup.

Bill Townsend coached at Economy from 1951 to '55. His best player was Jimmy Oler, a 1952 graduate who went on to play at Florida State.

At one time, there was a balcony that ran along the north side of the gym. It was little more than a wooden plank, accessible by a ladder along the east wall. "Peanut heaven," Tutterrow said.

"People would sit with their feet dangling over the balcony, dripping snow onto the people below," said Gene Himelick, who helps supervise the gym.

The high school team stopped using the gym for its home games after the 1957–58 season, instead playing at nearby Williamsburg. An independent team made up of local players called the Economy Royals played there from 1947 to '55.

"We played in gyms so small you couldn't even shoot a high-arcing shot," said Townsend, who went on to coach at Alquina, Fountain City and Lynn. "Those places were great. It was entertainment in those towns back then. You didn't have to be a parent or grandparent to go to the games. You could have had a catfight instead of a basketball game, and the same people would have come to watch."

The Economy gym was built in 1924. It is open each Wednesday night in the winter for an open gym.

The Economy gym once had a wooden plank along the north side that served as a balcony.

The gym floor at Economy is just sixty-one feet long. A regulation high school floor is eighty-four feet.

JASPER

Jasper's unlikely state championship in 1949 ranks right near the top of underdog stories in Indiana's high school basketball history.

Jasper entered the '49 sectional with an unremarkable 11-9 record. The Wildcats, though dangerous, were considered the third-best team in the sectional, behind Huntingburg—which owned two regular-season victories over Jasper—and undefeated Winslow, led by future Indiana University star Dick Farley.

"At lot of people over the years have asked why we were only 11-9 during the season," said Bob White, a five-foot-six senior that season. "Injuries played a part. And I think our coach, who was a god to me, was still feeling out his players. By the time the tournament came, we were able to make some assignment changes."

That coach was the legendary and colorful Leo "Cabby" O'Neill, who was in his tenth season and well on his way to establishing his legacy. White, who was inducted into the Indiana Basketball Hall of Fame in 2010 at age seventy-eight, called O'Neill "disciplined and demanding, yet full of idiosyncrasies."

"He was a little bit Jekyll and Hyde," White said. "After one game at Washington he drove all the way home and realized he forgot his wife. You could tease him about stuff like that, but he never wavered. His philosophy was that if you were disciplined and didn't deviate from your plan, the other team would eventually let down their guard."

In 1984, Jasper would name its former gym after O'Neill. Built at a cost of $100,000 in 1939 as a Work Projects Administration project, it seated thirty-two hundred fans. Fittingly, O'Neill's first game as coach at Jasper was the first one played in the gym. Jasper defeated Huntingburg 31–29 in overtime on November 3, 1939.

Jasper hosted the sectional in the gym every year from 1941 to '51, winning it eight times. That included the unlikely run in '49, when the Wildcats upset Huntingburg 44–35 in the semifinal and rallied from a ten-point halftime deficit to defeat Winslow 48–39.

It didn't stop there. Jasper won six more games, culminating with a 62–61 win over Madison in the state championship. White scored twenty points.

"Jasper was flying high when we won that championship," White said. "It was one event after another. It goes by so fast that you don't even realize it."

Jasper built a new gym and new school in 1977, ending a four-decade era that saw the Wildcats go 348-106 in their home building. The gym continued to be a home for middle school teams until 2004. The adjoining school was torn down in the summer of 2009, but a fundraising group raised enough money to convince the school board to save the gym.

There are preliminary plans for Jasper to play an occasional "throwback" game there.

"That would be a lot of fun," said Rick Begle, who scored the last basket at the gym in 1977. "I think we lost something from that era when we moved to the new gym."

An exterior look at the Cabby O'Neill gym in Jasper. It was built in 1939 as a Work Projects Administration project.

The school next to the Jasper gym was torn down, but the community rallied to save the gym.

BOURBON

Larry Lemler didn't graduate from Bourbon High School. He dropped out after the eighth grade to help run his father's meat locker in downtown Bourbon.

That was more than fifty years ago. Lemler is still running the business in the Marshall County community. And he's more than made up for his regretful decision to drop out of school, accumulating a treasure of Bourbon High School memorabilia that he proudly displays in a large room at his house, less than a mile east of where the school once sat.

Each year, Bourbon's fiftieth-anniversary class has its reunion at Lemler's house.

"My dad was a collector," he said. "I've always enjoyed talking to people and accumulating things."

Lemler, sixty-eight, doesn't claim a favorite among his many collections. But a large photo, displayed prominently above many other composite class portraits and team photos, attracts a visitor's eye. Forever captured in time, it shows the twelve members of the 1962 Bourbon basketball team celebrating its final sectional championship. The following year, the school consolidated with Etna Green and Tippecanoe to form Triton, which is located in Bourbon.

"We had a bunch of really good athletes that year," said Dick Campbell, eighty, who coached at Bourbon from 1957 to 1963.

"We won the country tournament, too, and had to beat Plymouth in the sectional [semifinal], which was the home team and a bigger school."

That Bourbon team made its home at a 1928 gym, considered a crown jewel when it was built. It was constructed after a fire destroyed the old school, where the team played in a basement room.

Though the adjoining school has since been torn down, the brick gym still stands and gets frequent use for Triton's elementary school practices. The bleachers on the north side of the gym were taken out to allow for extra space, and the two baskets placed on the north wall were taken out of Etna Green's gym, which has since been demolished. The south side includes a high wall, typical of gyms built at the time, and five rows of bleachers.

Among Lemler's collections is a small, blue wooden box, with "Comets" painted in white on one side. In the days before coaches could talk to players during timeouts, the coach would roll the towel box onto the floor, sometimes with a note written inside for the players.

"I had no idea," Lemler said. "That was a new one to me."

Lemler is still learning. And through his extensive collection, and the still-standing brick gym, it's possible to tangibly relive the past in Bourbon.

An exterior look at the 1928 Bourbon gym in Marshall County.

The Bourbon gym is used for elementary school basketball practices.

Larry Lemler has an extensive collection of Bourbon school memorabilia, including this black and white photo of the 1962 sectional championship team.

WAVELAND

Almost famous.

In 1985, Angelo Pizzo was an unknown writer and producer from Bloomington looking for a location to shoot his first film, about a small-town Indiana school winning a state basketball championship.

Pizzo found his location in Waveland, a community of 460 people in the southwest corner of Montgomery County.

"We were looking for one location where we could shoot it all," Pizzo said. "The school, the downtown square, the gym—all of it. We found the perfect place at Waveland."

There was a problem. Waveland had passed a bond to tear down the old high school, then used as an elementary school, and build a new one. Unable to convince the Waveland community leaders to hold off on the project for a year, Pizzo said, "It was on to 'Plan B.'"

Knightstown (gym), New Richmond (downtown) and Nineveh (since-demolished school) were picked to make up the composite community of Hickory in the movie *Hoosiers*.

"I don't blame Waveland," Pizzo said. "I understand it. They didn't know who we were and didn't know how the movie would end up. We weren't from a big studio."

Although it's difficult to imagine *Hoosiers* without the Knightstown gym, Waveland's 1937 gym would have been a capable alternative. It remains in pristine condition, with its original wood floor and glass backboards donated by the graduating class in 1951. The new elementary school was built around the gym in 1986, the same year *Hoosiers* was released.

"I don't recall all that was said back then, but I know we already had plans to build the new school," said Glen Livesay, who was on the school board at the time. "It just didn't work out."

From 1949 to 1953, the Waveland Hornets were as good as any small school team, winning sectionals four times. Under coach Cliff Davis, the 1951 Waveland team went 25-0 before losing 50–49 to Covington in the regional final at Clinton.

"There was God and there was Clifford Davis in Waveland," said Don Whitecotton, a starting guard on the '51 team. "Sometimes that order was reversed."

Keith Greve was a star of the '51 team. He went on to start four years at Butler under Tony Hinkle and was later inducted into the Indiana Basketball Hall of Fame.

"He was probably only six one in high school but was a big kid for that day and age," Whitecotton said.

With just a few rows of bleachers on each side, Whitecotton said the Waveland gym seated "maybe five hundred people." It was last used as a high school gym in 1971; the school consolidated with Ladoga and New Market to form Southmont that year.

Whitecotton, seventy-six, recently toured the gym with his son, Mike.

"It's such a neat little place," he said, "and still in really good condition. It reminded me of those days when they'd have chili suppers before our games on Friday nights and the whole town would be there."

The producers of the movie *Hoosiers* had designs on using the 1937 Waveland gym in Montgomery County as the home of the Hickory Huskers.

The Waveland Hornets enjoyed a remarkable run of success from 1949 to 1953.

STILESVILLE

Ann King Cummings only saw the inside the Stilesville gym one time. It was in 1985, at an all-school parade celebrating the last year the school was in use. The following year, elementary students were bussed to a new school in neighboring Amo.

Ann toured the gym with her newlywed husband, Jim Cummings, a six-foot-four rock of a center for the Stilesville Tigers of the mid-1950s. Ann had heard the stories before. A few rows of bleachers on each side. A stage on one end. The locker room underneath the stage. And that floor. Not a dead spot to be found. Jim loved that floor.

Cummings grew up a dirt-poor son of a tenant farmer two miles southeast of Stilesville just off State Highway 40 in Hendricks County. He was a natural athlete. Cummings ran hurdles for Stilesville's track team. Stilesville didn't even have hurdles to use for practice.

"He was my best player," said Lloyd Cooper, who coached Cummings for three years. "I used him as a guard his freshman year, and he learned to handle the ball. By his junior year we had him playing inside where he really belonged."

Stilesville's gym was built in 1938, the same year Cummings was born. Led by Ron McCammack, who went on to play at DePauw, the Tigers won the Hendricks County championship in 1950. The Tigers won the county again in '55 and might have had their best team in '56, when McCammack came back to coach, replacing Cooper.

Stilesville advanced to the championship game of the Danville Sectional that year with wins over Plainfield and North Salem. Danville defeated Stilesville 59–58 in the championship game, denying the Tigers their first sectional championship. The school would never win one, consolidating with Amo and Clayton to form Cascade in 1964.

"Even to this day, people say they got screwed," Ann Cummings said. "They've never forgotten that game."

Today, the gym is all that's left. The school was torn down, and a town hall and fire department now occupy the land where it once stood. The gym was used as an antique mall for several years, until Josh Reitzel bought the building in 2004. It's utilized for storage for his rental company.

The original goals are still attached at each end, and a yellow "S" remains visible at midcourt, tangible signs of its basketball days.

On March 22, 2009, Jim Cummings died of cancer. For many years after he graduated, Cummings played independent basketball in little towns all over the state. He never forgot his favorite place, though. Before he was buried, Ann Cummings made sure that a small piece of the of the Stilesville gym floor—about the size of a blackboard eraser—was placed next to him in the casket.

"That was such a special part of him," Ann said. "He played so many games there, and I know people loved to watch him play. He wasn't Rick Mount, but for this little town he was a big star."

The "S" is still visible at midcourt and the original baskets still hang in the 1938 Stilesville gym, which has been used for storage by a rental company since 2004. The school has been torn down.

The Stilesville gym was used as an antique mall for several years before Josh Reitzel bought the building in 2004.

VALLONIA

The oversized, color team photo of the 1950 Vallonia Redbirds hangs over one of the east doors inside the gym like it was placed there for a movie shoot. It just fits perfectly.

But in reality, and a forgotten fact even in Vallonia, the 1950 sectional championship team (the only one in school history) didn't play its games in the gym. It was dedicated on December 6, 1950, nine months after Vallonia defeated Seymour and Brownstown on the same day to win the Seymour Sectional.

"That picture's been up there so long even the people in Vallonia think we played there," said Russell Plummer, who averaged thirteen points as a senior in 1949–50.

From 1935 to 1950, the Redbirds didn't have a home. In January 1935, a fire destroyed the "Basketball Hall," a wood-frame building where the Jackson County school teams once played. It had a seventy-foot-long court but was just thirty feet wide, and the ceiling was just eighteen feet high. It was also situated near a creek, which proved advantageous at times.

"When you had to go to the restroom you could just turn around in the side door and pee in the creek," said Joe Peters, a 1948 Vallonia graduate.

Taxpayers turned down initiatives for a new gym until it was finally passed in late 1949. But that was too late for the 1949–50 team, which played its home games—and had for several years—at the Freeman Field Air Force Base near Seymour, more than ten miles away. Through the years, the Redbirds also practiced and occasionally played games at Medora, but the Freeman Field, with its potbellied stove, was their home.

"They had a very nice gym there," said Robert Kinnick, a substitute on the 1950 team. "We practiced there and got used to making it our home."

The new gym, a brick building with seven rows of bleachers on each side and a stage on the east end, took less than eight months to construct. The high school team used it for only twelve years before Vallonia was consolidated into Brownstown in 1962 (and became Brownstown Central with three other schools in 1964).

But the later teams, even with the new gym, couldn't recapture the magic of 1950. That season Vallonia went on to beat Mitchell—which had defeated eventual state champion Madison during the season—33–30 in the first game of the Bedford Regional.

"Going into the Bedford gym was like playing in Madison Square Garden to us," Plummer said. "That was a thrill of a lifetime."

As of July 2010, Plummer still visited once a month with the coach of that team, Hubert Bastil.

"He gets a little confused these days," Plummer said, "but if you get him talking about that team, he won't stop."

Above: An exterior look at the Vallonia gym.

Below: This gym in Vallonia was built in 1950. Before that, the team played at Freeman Air Force Base near Seymour. The Jackson County gym is now available for rent.

GAS CITY

Long before coaching at powerhouse Marion in the 1960s, Jack Colescott played for the fast-breaking Gas City Tigers of the late 1940s. Inside Gas City's tiny home gym, a fast break was at times a risky proposition.

"You had to be careful going in there too fast," said Colescott, who coached at Marion for six years, leading the Giants to the state championship game in 1968 and '69. "You'd put one foot up on the mat as you went in for a layup or you'd run into the wall. Those big heavy mats came in handy."

Colescott played on the last Gas City team of 1948, which finished 23-2. The next year, Gas City and neighboring Jonesboro consolidated to form Mississinewa.

Until 1950, Mississinewa played its home games in the 1923 gym, which was saved from demolition in 2002 and is presently used as an exercise room for residents of the adjoining apartment complex. The classrooms from the former school make up the apartments.

A hallway leading from the school to the gym recalls Gas City's proud basketball history, with newspaper clippings and photos of teams from the 1940s. Under coach Wilbur Cummins—a former Purdue star—Gas City didn't lose a home game from 1938 to 1940 and went 23-1 in 1940, losing to Marion 30–22 in the sectional championship.

Under Cummins, Gas City won its first sectional title in 1944 and again in '46, when the Tigers were among the last eight teams in the state still playing.

"Cummins had a really good ten-year tenure," Colescott said. "We used a zone to keep the other team from scoring, and we liked to run the break."

Fans entered the gym through a ramp that descends to the floor though an entrance on the north side of the building. Parents and adults sat on the north side of the gym, which featured permanent wood bleachers and a balcony. On the opposite side was a stage, where the student block sat on portable bleachers. The stage was also used for numerous class plays and graduation programs, as well as concerts and shows performed by clubs and employees of the Owens-Illinois Glass Company.

The gym remains in good condition. Though a tile floor has replaced the original wood floor, it's not difficult to imagine how the gym must have looked in those glory years of the 1940s.

"When the consolidation happened in 1948, the initial reaction was that it would never last," Colescott said. "Gas City and Jonesboro didn't have any love for each other. People said they'd never come to the games again. But when they started winning as Mississinewa, they came back. It's a basketball town."

The Gas City gym, built in 1923, now has a tile floor.

The former Gas City school in Grant County is now used for apartments. Newspaper clippings of Gas City's teams are in the hallway leading to the gym.

Students filled the Gas City gym for a pep rally. This photo is in a hallway outside the gym.

PARIS CROSSING

Though it didn't have its own sanctioned tournament until the 1975–76 school year, girls' basketball was played competitively in Indiana several decades earlier.

Gert Sullivan has proof: team photos of the Paris Crossing girls from the early 1930s that included her mother, Christine Darin.

"She always talked about how much she loved to play," said Sullivan, thumbing through a scrapbook.

In those early days of basketball, the Paris Crossing teams played in a small wood gym with a few rows of bleachers on one side and a wood-burning stove.

"In the southeast corner of the gym, the cold air would come in and the floor would 'sweat,'" said Paul Green, a 1948 graduate. "It was hazardous. You'd be slipping and sliding all over the place."

An arsonist burned the gym to the ground in 1949, and a new gym—located on a hill about a mile east of the former gym—was erected in 1953. Paris Crossing defeated Tampico 55–42 on December 11, 1953, in the Pirates' first game in their new home.

With just three rows of bleachers on either side, the new gym was hardly much bigger than the old one. During the fall of 1953, boys in physical education classes worked to get the gym prepared, putting up the backboards, hanging the scoreboard and painting the bleachers. Before it was game ready, the Paris Crossing teams would practice on a dirt court west of the school or use Vernon's gym, depending on the weather.

The gym was connected to the school (since torn down) by a downstairs tunnel. There were bathroom and locker rooms in the basement, considered a luxury. The large windows on the north and south sides of the gym have since been filled in with concrete blocks.

Paris Crossing's first two teams in the new gym were probably its best. The 1953–54 team went 16-2 and lost to perennial power and much larger Madison 94–84 in the sectional semifinals.

"We only went about five deep, but we had a pretty good little team," said Harold "Mo" Callahan, a 1955 graduate. "That gym got there just in time. We always had people lined up all the way around the court to watch."

The Pirates went 17-5 in 1954–55, losing to Madison again in the sectional semifinals.

After several years as an elementary school, the town bought the gym in 1970. For twenty dollars an hour, the gym is still available to rent.

"We don't get the amount of people we used to, but there are a lot of regulars," said Glen Sullivan, a local resident who maintains the gym.

The building was last used as a high school gym in 1960–61. The next year, the school was consolidated into Vernon.

An exterior look at the Paris Crossing gym. An arsonist burned down the previous gym.

This 1955 gym in Paris Crossing is available to rent. When it was a high school gym, spectators would line up along the wall to watch the games.

LITTLE YORK

Visitors approaching the Washington County village of Little York from the north on Indiana 39 might mistake the white structure with the arched roof for a barn typical of those dotting the rolling countryside of southern Indiana.

Take a closer look. Through the open doors on the east side of the building, the morning sun illuminates a backboard hanging from a metal standard attached to the ceiling. The wood floor has been torn out, and the five rows of wood bleachers are littered with stray boards and random pieces of machinery.

This was a gym at one time; a community center built in 1936 as a Works Progress Administration project. There was no electricity in the building. The gym was heated by two coal-burning stoves, one in the northwest corner and the other in the southeast corner.

"I remember playing one game in there, and you could see your breath," said Lee Jackson, class of 1941. "It was 19 degrees."

The first Little York Wildcats were part of the Indiana High School Athletic Association beginning in 1921. The first basketball teams played on the second floor of a general store. After the new community center was built, the high school teams played there until the school was absorbed by Salem in 1947.

"We had a class of seventeen—boys and girls," said Jackson, eighty-six, interviewed in February 2010. "That was a pretty big class."

Little York had an elementary school until 1967. Jackson, who owned the adjacent property and still lives one hundred yards to the south, bought the school and the gym from the Salem school corporation. For many years, locals used the gym for pickup games.

"There got to be too many fights, and everything would get torn up," Jackson said. "So I took down the basket on one end so they couldn't play in there anymore."

Larry Martin, Jackson's son-in-law, built a house on the foundation where the school once sat. In 2009, with the roof sagging on the old gym, Martin paid a group of Amish workers to have it fixed.

Martin still gets an occasional visitor asking for a tour. More often, he'll notice a car drive by slowly.

"Hopefully it'll last a while longer," Martin said. "I don't know if it will or not. I always tell people I'm going to turn it into a nightclub."

Opposite, top: The Little York gym in Washington County was built in 1936 and resembles a barn.

Opposite, bottom left: A backboard still hangs from the 1936 gym in Little York.

Opposite, bottom right: The former Little York gym was heated by two coal-burning stoves.

VERNON

Completed in 1941 as a Work Projects Administration project, the former high school gym at Vernon in Jennings County is enjoying a busy afterlife.

"We're busy here pretty much seven days a week," said Danny Stark, a Vernon town board member who oversees the day-to-day operations of the gym. "We always have something going on."

The Vernon gym is a true "community center." There are five classrooms on the north side of the building that are rented out for $150 a month and used for dance classes, a weight room, karate classes and other programs for children. Another room, just off to the right as you enter the north doors, honors Vernon's history with class photos, letter jackets and even score books from basketball games in the 1940s, '50s and '60s.

Harry Stewart, seventy-five, played and coached in many of those games. A 1953 Vernon graduate, Stewart was the first player in Jennings County to score one thousand points. After college, he came back to coach the blue-and-gold Vernon Blue Devils from 1957 to 1964. Vernon was consolidated into North Vernon in '64 and became known as Jennings County in '68.

"That gym probably only seated three hundred people, but it was one of the nicest ones around," Stewart said. "There were a few rows of bleachers on both sides,

and the band and some people sat up on the stage."

The windows on both the east and west sides have been filled in with concrete blocks to save on heating costs, but the look of the gym remains mostly unchanged. The dark floors add to the old-time feel.

Bob Barber, who still lives in Vernon, was the captain of the 1962–63 team.

"One of my favorite memories of that gym was in 1961, and we were playing New Marion," he said. "Their coach was very volatile and animated, kind of like [former Indiana coach] Bob Knight. They also had a really good player named Gene Demaree, who was an Indiana all-star [in 1961] and played at Indiana. Well, during the game, the coach got upset at a call and slung his coat jacket. It got stuck on one of the rafters, and they had to stop the game to get it down. You didn't see that happen every day."

Vernon had some good teams, including a 16-4 season in Stewart's senior year of 1952–53. But playing in the Greensburg Sectional for many years against bigger schools like Greensburg and North Vernon, the Blue Devils never won a sectional.

"We had a lot of great memories in that gym," Barber said. "It was a great environment for basketball. I always looked forward to that first practice when we'd get our white Chuck Taylor tennis shoes."

An exterior look at the former Vernon gym.

The Vernon gym was built through the Work Projects Administration in 1941. It is now part of a community center and is busy almost every night of the week.

DUPONT

It's a Friday night in February, and the Dupont gym is jumping, just like it was seventy years ago. There isn't as much on the line for these fifth and sixth graders, but at least it's basketball.

There's a concession stand in the northwest corner of the gym, and the smell of popcorn fills the air. A yellow curtain with a black "D" is drawn on the west end, where the high school once had its graduations and school plays. The rock walls add a unique touch.

"It's about as solidly built a place as you'll ever see," said Lee Carlisle, a 1962 graduate and truck driver who still lives in Dupont. "I think that thing would hold up to a tornado or a hurricane."

Not that there are any plans to attempt to tear it down. Though the school consolidated into Madison in 1965, the gym—built in 1938 as a Works Progress Administration project—continues to serve the students of the attached elementary school and is used for various community functions.

"It's in really good shape," Carlisle said. "It looks pretty much like it did thirty or forty years ago."

Stan Nay's first job out of college, at age twenty-one in 1960, was as the head coach at Dupont. At that time, the school—which housed grades one through twelve—was a brick building just off State Highway 7 in the Jefferson County community of about four hundred people. The gym was built behind the school, unattached and several yards to the west.

When the old school was torn down, the new elementary school connected to the gym.

"It was very small, but it was a small school and met our needs," said Nay, who eventually left coaching and became superintendent at Versailles. "I was invited back there for an alumni event four or five years ago and was impressed with how it looked."

There were a few rows of bleachers on each side of the court, and Nay remembers that the community was always supportive. Unfortunately, they never had much to cheer about, and the coaches usually shuffled through every two or three years. During Nay's two seasons, from 1960 to 1962, Dupont was 12-29.

Carlisle's senior year, the Hornets played against Indiana Mr. Basketball Larry Humes and Madison in the first round of the sectional. Madison won, 83–35.

"We were just a bunch of country boys," Carlisle said. "Going to play Larry Humes and Madison was David and Goliath. But we always had a good following in that old gym. It wasn't the fault of our fan base."

Dupont's gym features visible rock on the interior. The adjoining elementary school uses the gym for games and practices.

An exterior look at the Dupont gym in Jefferson County.

The Dupont gym was built in 1938 as a Works Progress Administration project.

NEWPORT

For one dollar an hour—if you're at least eighteen—you can shoot hoops in one of the oldest gyms still standing in Vermillion County, near the Illinois border.

The former Newport gym, built in 1925, is now part of the Vermillion County Public Library system. The gym is located in the downstairs portion of the former school, and the library, which moved into the old school in 1991, is upstairs.

The basement location, with the Wabash River nearby, turned out to be less than ideal. The gym has been flooded and the wood floor replaced three times.

When it was used for high school games (until 1964, when it consolidated with Cayuga and Perrysville into North Vermillion), the players sat on the stage on the south side. On the opposite side is a wide concrete balcony where fans would stand along the railing to watch games. There were chairs set up underneath the balcony, and fans would also stand around the perimeter of the court.

"That balcony was usually filled," said Jack Burroughs, a 1948 graduate. "You'd look up there, and there were people trying to peek over other people's shoulders to see."

Though the gym mostly sits in silence now, it still fills up twice a year—once in June for a school reunion and again at the end of September for the "Queen Contest," which runs in conjunction with the Newport Lions Club Antique Auto Hill Climb, a three-day festival and an annual event for more than forty years.

Despite the flooding problems, the Newport gym persevered, unlike the gym at neighboring Cayuga, which was built in a similar style with the balcony overlooking the floor on one side. Though the out-of-bounds lines ran right up against the walls, Burroughs said that wasn't unusual for that time.

"Wallace [in Fountain County] had one with three big ol' stoves that was a big furnace," he said. "It looked like a barn. We played in some small places."

Burroughs had eleven boys and five girls in his graduating class, a small group even by Newport's standards. The red-and-white Newport Tigers never won a sectional, as host Clinton normally dominated the smaller county schools.

Pam Hazelwood, the library director, went to school at Newport through her sophomore year in 1964 and graduated from North Vermillion in 1966.

"I saw lots of basketball games in here," she said. "We still have groups that rent it out regularly, which helps keep it alive."

Opposite, top: The Newport gym is in what is now a library in Vermillion County.

Opposite, bottom: Fans stood on this platform above the floor in the 1925 Newport gym to watch games.

MARION

From 1963 to 1970, Mike Jenkins shared an "organ loft" inside the Marion Coliseum with Bill Fowler, the play-by-play radio voice for the Marion Giants on WBAT.

The lofts—situated about eight feet of the ground on both sides of the stage on the north end of the court—were used as a quasi radio booth. Jenkins and Fowler broadcasted games from the loft on the east side of the stage.

"Judging the trajectory of the ball wasn't easy from that angle," Jenkins said. "It was a little different, but you got used to being at the end of the court."

Fowler, a member of the 1940 Indiana All-Star Team, played for Adolph Rupp at Kentucky for a year but had his career interrupted by World War I. He returned to Marion and became an institution as the voice of the Giants for more than thirty years.

"He was the ultimate Marion backer," Jenkins said. "Sometimes during games he would stand up and yell at the officials. But mechanically, he was a great play-by-play guy. You could close your eyes and know just what was happening on the court."

Surprisingly, despite its seven state championships, not one of those teams played its home games at the Marion Coliseum, where the Giants played from 1928 to 1970. But the coliseum did host many sectional and regional tournaments through the years, many of those won by the home team. The Giants won ten regional tournaments at the coliseum.

Marion regularly filled its more than five thousand seats for basketball games and also packed the coliseum every year for the Marion Easter Pageant, which started in 1937.

"The Marion Coliseum was a basketball monument," said Jim Sutter, a 1952 Marion graduate. "It was built during that time when basketball was red-hot and a lot of cities were building bigger gyms."

After the high school team moved out in 1970, the coliseum was relegated to part-time use.

"It wasn't in very good shape, even those last few years Marion played there," Jenkins said. "The locker rooms were in rough condition, and there was a problem with bats."

In 1998, the City of Marion purchased the coliseum from the school for $1. In 2004, the YMCA bought the coliseum from the city for $2 and began its massive renovation, which cost an estimated $9 million.

Though the inside of the coliseum looks much different, there are reminders of the old gym. On one wall is the old midcourt—a purple circle with a yellow "M"—encased in a glass box. The green bleachers in the second deck on the west side are the same as when it was built, as are the signs marking each section with a letter. And the organ lofts—they are still there, too.

In the year since the YMCA moved to Marion Coliseum, membership has tripled. The boom is in part due to the new additions—a large weight room and three swimming pools, among them—but also because of its connection to the past.

"What's been done here with the coliseum will never be duplicated," Sutter said. "There might be others that are just as nice but not with the history this place has."

An outside look
at the Marion
Coliseum,
built in 1928.
After extensive
renovation, the
YMCA now uses
the gym. Marion
had four teams
reach the state finals
in the time it played
in the coliseum.

The Marion
Coliseum at one
time seated more
than five thousand
fans and hosted
sectional and
regional games for
many years. The
Marion Giants
moved out in 1970.

HARRISBURG

As a member of the nearby Orange High School basketball team, Malcolm Geise played in the first game at the new Harrisburg gym in Fayette County in 1930.

"I scored fifteen points, and Harrisburg had fourteen," said Geise, a 1932 Orange graduate.

Geise, interviewed in March 2010 at age ninety-five, later became a school bus driver at Harrisburg and kept the score book at basketball games for eighteen years, beginning in 1940. The scorer's table was located on the floor—the original dark brown tile floor has been replaced twice—with the home and visiting team benches on each side.

A balcony wrapped around three sides of the gym with a stage on the east end. The three-story school that was once attached to the gym has since been replaced with a new school, now Fayette Central Elementary.

"At one time there were theater-style seats in the balcony," said Dave Simpkins, maintenance director at the school. "There probably aren't too many around that still have balconies. They talked about taking this one down when they put in new plumbing, but they never did."

Upon entering the gym through the west doors, there are two staircases—one on the left and one on the right—that lead up to the balcony. Geise said he remembers "kids running around up there" at games in the 1940s and '50s. Other spectators either sat in folding chairs on the floor around the court or on portable bleachers on the stage.

Harrisburg had several good teams through the 1940s and '50s, including a 20-3 record in 1952–53 under coach Cecil Tague, an Indiana Basketball Hall of Famer who also coached at Whitewater Township, Milroy, Spiceland and New Castle.

Harrisburg took students from the north end of Connersville, a neighborhood called Beeson's Addition that sprang up after World War II. Jake Bradburn, one of the best players on the 1952–53 team, was one of those from the neighborhood. He died a few years later in the Korean War.

"Some of our best players came from Beeson's Addition," Tague said. "Harrisburg was just a rural community three or four miles from Connersville, but there were some pretty good players around there."

Connersville annexed Beeson's Addition in the late 1950s, and in 1958, Harrisburg consolidated with Orange and Fairview to form Fayette Central. The Fayette Central Chiefs continued to use the Harrisburg gym until 1966, when Connersville became the only high school in the county.

"It's still a great little gym, and the kids get a lot of use out of it," Simpkins said. "It probably doesn't look all that different than it did in 1930."

Above: The 1930 Harrisburg gym in Fayette County featured a wraparound balcony on three sides. Team members would run up the steps and around the balcony for workouts.

Opposite, inset: An exterior shot of the Harrisburg gym. It is now part of an elementary school.

DECATUR CATHOLIC

Dave Terveer, eighty-five, played in an era before the Indiana High School Athletic Association allowed Catholic schools to compete in the state tournament.

"We had fifteen or sixteen Catholic schools in the state, and we'd all play in the state Catholic tournament," Terveer said. "In 1941, we upset Cathedral in the first round. I still have that program from all those years ago."

Decatur Catholic, along with the state's other Catholic schools, was allowed to compete alongside the other Indiana high schools by 1943, a year after Terveer graduated. It wasn't until 1966, a year before the high school closed, that Decatur Central won a sectional championship.

That team—and many before it, dating back to the mid-'50s—played only road games. Decatur Catholic's tiny gym, built with the school in 1925, was too cramped to accommodate a crowd of much more than three hundred people. On one side of the floor were several rows of theater-style seats, and on the other, there was a balcony with several more rows of bleachers.

"We had good crowds, and we could get them in there, but we needed a bigger playing spot," said Terveer, who coached basketball and taught at the school from 1948 to 1956. "It was quite a bit smaller than a standard floor."

The former high school is now an elementary school, and the gym is fully functional. The original wood gym floor has been replaced by a rubber surface.

Early in his tenure as coach, Terveer worked to coordinate the schedule so that

Decatur Catholic could play its games at the Decatur High School gym, located just two blocks away.

"We played Lancaster Central one time on a Sunday afternoon," Terveer said with a laugh. "Sometimes we just couldn't work around their schedule. But I finally got to a point where I would get their schedules ahead of time and make ours fit."

Into the 1960s, the Commodores continued to practice in their home gym, using the Decatur gym once a week. One of the unique features of the gym—other than the balcony, which has since been walled off—was a big homemade electric scoreboard in one corner. On hooks under the "home" and "visitor" signs, the players' names were written on a piece of paper.

In 1956, Terveer left the teaching and coaching profession for a job at General Electric—"better pay," he said—and stayed for thirty years. Decatur Catholic won the sectional in 1966 under coach Bob Boyle, who had a part in the 1986 movie *Hoosiers* as a referee. His son, Brad Boyle, played the role of Whit Butcher in

the movie, one of the players for the fictional 1952 state champion Hickory Huskers.

The '66 Decatur Catholic team upset Ossian, the fifth-ranked team in the state, in the sectional championship. John Lose, a senior and leading scorer on the team, still has the audiotape of the game from WADM-AM out of Decatur.

"We weren't supposed to beat them," Lose said. "But we were used to playing road games. We didn't play a home game all through high school."

Above: Beginning in the 1950s, Decatur Catholic had to play its games on the road because this gym was too small. It was built in 1925.

Opposite, inset: An exterior look at the Decatur Catholic gym.

DECATUR

As a young boy in the early 1950s, Bob Shraluka remembers walking through the snow to the school in the center of Decatur. It was a bustling downtown then, like many small Indiana communities.

"It had everything you could imagine," said Shraluka, now sixty-nine. "There were jewelry stores, restaurants and movie theaters. It was a booming little town."

The heart of the community—in more ways than one—were the school and gymnasium, built in 1938. One of the biggest gyms in Adams County, Decatur hosted the sectional until 1952, when Adams Central built its new gym.

One of the unique features of the Decatur gym, although not all that uncommon for gyms of its time, is a brick wall that surrounds the gym floor, just three feet from the inbounds line.

"It's kind of crazy, isn't it?" Shraluka said. "You could crash right into that wall so easily. I guess we didn't even think about it back then."

The gym was the home of the Decatur Yellow Jackets until 1967, when the school consolidated with Decatur Catholic and Monmouth to become Bellmont. The Bellmont Braves used the gym and the school—a crowded school—through the 1969–70 school year.

"You could barely walk through the hallways," said Dave Meyer, a 1968 Bellmont grad.

Except for a storage area on top of the bleachers on one side of the gym, it remains relatively unchanged from 1970. Painted on one side of the stage in horizontal letters is "Braves," the Bellmont nickname. On the other side is "Squaws," the nickname of the girls' teams.

The gym is now part of the Adams County Service Complex and is open to the public for recreation. The cost is just $2 for a day or $125 for an entire year. There are basketball leagues and volleyball leagues, as well as a separate fitness center and weight room.

The school and classrooms are now used for various county offices. It remains a hub of activity, just for different purposes than in the 1940s, '50s and '60s. While other Adams County gyms in Berne and Geneva were torn down in 2010, there are no plans to get rid of the former Decatur gym or school.

"They take good care of it," said Shraluka, who helped lead Decatur to a sectional title (its last before consolidation) as a senior in 1959. "I know guys in their seventies who go over there and shoot around."

Opposite, top: An exterior look at the Decatur gym.

Opposite, bottom: The gym in Decatur was one of the biggest in Adams County when it was built in 1938. It is now part of the Adams County Service Complex and is used for basketball and volleyball leagues.

SHELBYVILLE

With three black players in its starting lineup, it wasn't unusual for Shelbyville to endure bigoted catcalls at road venues during the 1946–47 season. But for Shelbyville fans, the overt racism finally came to a head on January 3, 1947, in front of a sellout crowd of thirty-five hundred inside its own Paul Cross Gym.

It was a matchup between two of the state's top teams and two of its top players in six-foot-ten Terre Haute Garfield star Clyde Lovellette and Shelbyville's Bill Garrett. In addition to Garrett, who would go on to be named Indiana's Mr. Basketball, Shelbyville coach Frank Barnes also started the two other black players on the team, Emerson Johnson and Marshall Murray.

Though the team had been integrated for several years, it was the first time Shelbyville started three black players.

"They were the best players," said Don Robinson, a junior on the '47 team. "As kids, we didn't think anything of it. You heard something on the road, but at home, I think our fans became pretty protective of our team."

Case in point was the game against Terre Haute Garfield. The partisan Shelbyville crowd felt that referee Earl Townsend was making favorable calls for the all-white Garfield team, particularly against Garrett and Murray. When Garrett fouled out early in the fourth quarter of what became

An exterior look at Shelbyville's Paul Gross Gym. It was the site of an ugly incident in 1947.

a 52–44 loss, the fans exploded, screaming threats at Townsend and throwing debris onto the court.

"I was sitting right by [Barnes], and early in the game he said, 'I don't like what I'm seeing here,'" Robinson said of the calls. "When the game finally ended, he said, 'Run for the dressing room.'"

Several fans stormed the court, looking to get a piece of Townsend, who was quickly rushed off the court by police escort, along with colleague Don Veller, to a downstairs dressing room.

"It got a little wild at the end," said Bill Breck, a senior starter on the '47 team. "Fortunately, no one got hurt, and our school wasn't penalized for it."

Led by Garrett, Shelbyville went on to win the state championship in '47,

Shelbyville's gym was built in 1922. The Golden Bears played there until 1967.

defeating Terre Haute Garfield in the title game. Garrett went on to play at Indiana and, later, for the Harlem Globetrotters. He coached Crispus Attucks to the 1959 state title. Garrett died in 1974, at age forty-five, of severe heart arrhythmia.

"He was a gentleman," Breck said. "Bill took a lot of verbal abuse, and he was a very steady guy all the time. We probably didn't realize the things those guys heard at some places."

Shelbyville moved out of its 1922 Paul Cross Gym when a new gym was built—and later named for Garrett—in 1967. The old gym has been used as a civic center for the Shelbyville Parks and Recreation Department since 1997, hosting volleyball and basketball leagues, open gyms and various programs.

The stage on one end has been walled off, but the shell of the gym remains mostly unchanged, with permanent bleachers descending down from the darkness on both sides of the floor. In the early 2000s, Shelbyville played two games at the Paul Cross Gym when there were ventilation problems in the other one.

"Talk about a throwback atmosphere," Shelbyville athletic director Paul Heidenreich said. "A lot of people came out who hadn't been to a Shelbyville game in a long time."

BRYANT

The Bryant Owls played home games in the 1920s and '30s in a makeshift gym—a building with wooden posts in the middle of the court—located downtown in the Jay County community. That building served its purpose, but it wasn't sufficient as basketball continued to boom in the Hoosier state into the '40s.

In that decade, Bryant played its games at the armory in Portland until Ted Montgomery—a 1934 Bryant graduate—led a fundraising charge to build the Owls their own home. George Garlinger designed the gym, and its construction was truly a community effort. Students were even pulled out of study hall to help. The new gym was ready for the start of the 1951–52 season.

Almost immediately, it became obvious that the tile floor—a kitchen-style linoleum surface laid on top of a concrete base—was too slick.

"We did it to save some money," said Carl Hoehamer, a 1941 Bryant graduate who was a custodian when the gym was built and helped with its construction. "But it would sweat too much because of the humidity in the building."

It was replaced by a wood floor after the 1957–58 season, the same year the Owls won their first sectional championship. That team was led by junior Dick Masters, who would go on to play at Murray State. Masters was an athletic six-foot guard who scored 49 points in an 81–42 sectional win over the Gray Redbirds in 1959. He is Bryant's all-time leading scorer with 1,574 points.

"He was our big gun," said David Lyons, a 1960 Bryant graduate. "He could dunk and play about any position on the floor. He wasn't a nasty person, but he was a ferocious competitor."

Bryant's gym had four rows of bleachers on the north side and twelve rows on the south side with gravel underneath. The main entrance was on the west end, with a stage on the east and locker rooms under the stage.

The Owls won another sectional in 1963, led by coach John Minch, now the mayor of Berne. Bryant won the ten-team sectional at Hartford City that year, defeating Hartford City, Dunkirk, Madison Township and Redkey. Bryant won three of those games by a total of thirteen points.

"We were underdogs," said John Garlinger, a junior starter on that team. "Portland and Madison had bigger guys than we did, but we played pretty well together."

Bryant continued to produce winning teams through the 1975 season, when all of the remaining county schools were consolidated to form Jay County. The bleachers from Bryant were taken out and moved to the new school in Portland.

The Bryant school was torn down soon after, but the community rallied to save the gym. The Bryant Area Community Center is under the ownership of Bearcreek Township and is used for a variety of purposes, including church league basketball, reunions, card games and even weddings. The only dramatic change from the original building is a kitchen that has been added where the bleachers once sat on the south side.

"It gets a lot of use," Garlinger said. "There's something going on in that gym almost every day."

The Bryant Owls
moved out of
their smaller gym
and into this one
in 1951.

Now a community center, the former Bryant gym gets
a lot of use.

A photo inside the Bryant gym honors the 1963 sectional
championship team.

PLEASANTVILLE

With an enrollment of just forty-seven students in 1964–65, Pleasantville was the smallest high school in the state. When the team started the season with a 4-1 record, the *Evansville Courier* sent a reporter to Pleasantville to chronicle the Blue Streaks, who were playing their last season before consolidation sent students north to Union (Dugger).

"They did a full-page spread on us," said Terry Brady, who was in his second season as coach, taking the job as a twenty-one-year-old out of Indiana State. "We were a scrappy team that didn't have any size, but nobody wanted to play us."

Pleasantville had one of the more unique-looking gyms in the area to call home. With high-arching wood trusses stretching overhead, it gives the appearance of being much larger than its actual size. It was constructed in 1954, after community members voted that the former gym—located in the basement of the 1916 school—was not sufficient. The cost for the new building was about $70,000.

The 1955 Pleasantville yearbook proclaimed: "It fulfills a great community need and will serve the community for many years to come."

The first game was played in the new gym on February 11, 1955. The senior class only played two games in the new building before the end of the season. The team had been practicing and playing its "home" games in Carlisle, several miles west in Sullivan County.

"The old gym [at Pleasantville] had a concrete floor with a few rows of bleachers on one side and a balcony with a couple rows above it," said Jerry Abram, a senior on the '55 team. "They finally decided it was too dangerous for us to play there."

The new gym, which resembles a white barn from the outside, was constructed just to the west of the school. There were five rows of bleachers that stretched north to south on both sides of the court and large windows on the east and west. Capacity was about five hundred.

After several lean years, the Blue Streaks won fourteen games in each of the school's final two seasons. The gym was, and still is, a source of pride in tiny Pleasantville. Tonie Mejean, the wife of town trustee Frank Mejean, said it took her about ninety combinations of paint to get the right shade of blue to repaint the light blue circle around the "P" at midcourt.

"There weren't any gyms I saw that had those solid wood beams like ours," said Tucker Figg, a 1965 graduate.

The school has long since been torn down, but the gym—now owned by the town—is used for some community functions. Abram, seventy-three, played in it for several years after he graduated with independent league teams.

"The school really didn't get to use it all that long," Abram said. "They kept it up for many years after that, though. It fell into some disrepair, but they've done some work to it and it's functional again. There just aren't that many people in town to use it."

Above: Before this gym was built, the Pleasantville Blue Streaks played in the basement of the 1916 school.

Opposite, inset: An exterior look at the 1955 Pleasantville gym in Sullivan County. When the tiny school was consolidated, independent teams played there. It is now used by the community.

PENNVILLE

Pennville residents celebrated in style on October 13, 1953, to formally dedicate the completion of their new gym. An estimated crowd of seven hundred—nearly 100 percent of Pennville's population—turned out for the two-and-a-half-hour program, which included "a band, glitter, noted speakers and refreshments," according to the *Portland Commercial-Review*.

The new gym was truly a community project. Though the total cost was $110,000, an estimated $25,000 was saved because of the donated labor and equipment from Pennville residents. Whenever a new truckload of concrete blocks would arrive in town, the truck driver would honk his horn on the way to the gym to alert the townspeople.

"The gym was really a source of pride because of how much work was put into it," said Dean Monroe, a 1972 Pennville graduated who authored a book on Jay County basketball.

Prior to the construction of the new gym, which featured a rounded roof and four high windows on both the north and south sides with seating for about twelve hundred, the Pennville Bulldogs played their games in a 1916 building that resembled a white barn. There were potbellied stoves at each end of the court to heat it, although players had to run outside and to the school to get to the showers. The gym was used as a bus barn until the late 1960s.

Pennville enjoyed basketball success, winning sectionals in 1924, '35 and '42. The Bulldogs didn't win another sectional

until they made the new gym their home, breaking through in 1962 with a 58–57 overtime win over host Portland in the championship game.

That team was led by six-foot-seven Richard "Stretch" Davidson, who went on to play at Western Kentucky and came back to teach in the Randolph Southern school system for thirty-six years.

"We had a good following," Davidson said. "We'd get on the school bus and have a line of cars following us wherever we went. It's funny that gym seemed so big to us back then."

The gym remains in pristine condition today, used by the adjoining elementary school. On the south wall are banners of the former Jay County high schools: the Bryant Owls, Dunkirk Speedcats, Portland Panthers, Pennville Bulldogs, Madison Tomcats, Poling Yellow Jackets, Gray Redbirds and Redkey Wolves.

In 1975, Bryant, Dunkirk, Pennville, Portland and Redkey (Poling, Madison and Gray had already closed) were consolidated to form Jay County.

Pennville graduates gather in the gym every year for an alumni celebration and share old stories. Monroe has two favorites.

"In December 1964 we were playing Ossian," he said. "It was a wild game. There were sixty-three personal fouls and six technicals. Ossian got put on probation for it. In 1969, we were playing Fort Recovery [Ohio]. They had a really good team, but with about six minutes to go we were giving the Indians all they could handle. Then the lights go out. We wait for about fifteen minutes, and the lights came back on. We couldn't make a shot. We should have just left them off."

Above: The Pennville gym in Jay County was dedicated in 1953 and used by the high school team until 1975. It is now part of an elementary school.

Opposite, inset: An exterior look at the Pennville gym.

HOAGLAND

Hoagland had roughly the same enrollment in 1954 as Milan, the Bobby Plump–led small school team that won the state championship and inspired the movie *Hoosiers*. Hoagland didn't have nearly the same success in '54, finishing just 7-12.

"But we were there," said Bob Weller, a 1954 Hoagland graduate. "Some of us got tickets to Butler [Hinkle] Fieldhouse and went down for the games. By the time we got in, the game had started, but we were there for Plump's [game-winning] shot."

Hoagland struggled in '54, but the Wildcats enjoyed several good seasons playing in its 1926 gym. The standalone brick building seated about seven hundred people, with five rows of bleachers on both sides and a stage on the north end. Behind the basket on the south end, where fans entered the building from two entrances, there was a concession stand where fans would wait in line for popcorn and hot dogs.

"You would have to be careful in the pregame warm-ups because people would be standing right there with their back to you," Weller said. "It was easy to run right into them."

Hoagland never won a sectional, often times running up against bigger Fort Wayne schools in a huge sixteen-team field. The 1952 team, coached by Jim Chesnut, made it to the sectional semifinals. The '58 team, with Keith Bohnke at center, went 19-3 but lost to Concordia in the sectional.

"It was almost impossible for us smaller country schools to beat those city teams," said Jim Asby, a '52 graduate who operated Aspy Tire in Hoagland from 1954 to 1997. "It happened, but not very often."

Hoagland and rival Monroeville were consolidated to form Heritage in 1968.

"The communities hated each other," said Dick Stoppenhagen, a 1954 Hoagland grad. "It was hard for a lot of us old people to accept. We get along fine now, but there really wasn't any back and forth between the older people in the communities for a long time."

The old Hoagland school, built the same year as the gym, was torn down, and a new elementary school was constructed in the 1980s. The school is attached to the gym. The corridor between the school and gym includes old Hoagland class pictures and a "memory case" with trophies, letter jackets, band and cheerleader uniforms and even a Wildcat mascot costume. On a smaller scale, the display is similar to what could be found at the Indiana Basketball Hall of Fame.

The gym isn't exactly the same as it was when Hoagland's teams played there. The stage on the north end was taken out to allow for more floor space. On one March day, students had science fair projects spread all over the court and in the few rows of bleachers on both sides.

To Aspy, the gym represents a better era.

"I think people cared more about each other then than they do now," he said. "You think about how much those teams meant to the community here. You can't bring those days back."

A stage was taken out of the north end of the Hoagland gym to allow for more floor space.

An outside look at the 1926 Hoagland gym in Allen County.

A case of memorabilia outside the Hoagland gym. The gym is now used by the adjoining elementary school.

MECCA

Ray Wilson walked into the gym at the old Mecca High School recently and wondered aloud, "How in the devil did we play basketball in here?"

Wilson, class of 1958 at Mecca, isn't alone. The gym was built in 1923, attached to the east side of the 1901 schoolhouse. It is stunningly tiny. Along each side of the court—and barely out of bounds—are three white steel beams that protrude from the ceiling down to the wood floor. The black baselines are a mere two or three inches from the walls on each end. The bleachers have been taken out but once included five or six steep rows on both sides that stretched up to the windows.

This was Indiana high school basketball at its coziest.

"The bleachers were right up even to the floor," Wilson said. "There were mats wrapped around those posts so you wouldn't get hurt if you ran into them. It was so small and compact. There was nowhere to go."

This made it especially difficult for a referee attempting to escape a knife-wielding fan. According to Wilson, such a thing happened at Mecca in the early 1950s. Thankfully, cooler heads prevailed. But Wilson's father, Harley Wilson, won a battle of wits with a referee during a game against neighboring Bridgeton later in the 1950s. Lighting into a referee early and often that night, Harley Wilson earned the Arabs a technical foul. He wasn't done. Wilson took a seat on the south side of the gym—the Bridgeton side—and continued to tear into the officials, earning Bridgeton a technical. All even.

"We had some rowdy fans," Ray Wilson said with a laugh.

Mecca, a community of about 350 people located off the beaten path in western Parke County, lost its high school in 1963. The school was absorbed by Montezuma, five miles north. The elementary school lasted until 1986, when it was also closed. The town bought it from the Riverton Parke school corporation for one dollar, keeping it alive as a community center for several years. In February 2007, a nonprofit group called the Mecca ARABS (Mecca Alliance Representing A Building Savoir) formed to raise money for necessary upgrades and repairs.

The group received a $212,000 grant from the state, and repairs were made in the summer of 2009 that included a new roof for the school, new gutters, insulation and wiring.

"We've done a lot to raise money," said Ronnie Sanders, who attended school at Mecca through his sophomore year in '63. "We have car shows, bowl-a-thons, a food shack at the county fair. We have a group of about 110 people that really care about keeping it up."

Sanders said the group plans to add a section of bleachers that would replicate the originals.

"It was small, but it was probably one of the best in the county," Sanders said. "Bridgeton had a low ceiling. You couldn't arch the ball too much. Other than Rockville and Marshall, Mecca's gym might have been the biggest around."

The Mecca gym, built in 1923, featured three steel beams on each side of the floor.

The Mecca gym in Parke County was built on to the school, which was built in 1901. The elementary school was there until 1986.

An exterior look at the Mecca gym. A nonprofit group called the Mecca ARABS has raised money for repairs and improvements to the gym and school.

PINE VILLAGE

The post–Depression era gyms built as Work Projects Administration projects had style. There was no cookie-cutter pattern. An example was the Pine Village gym, built in 1940. Wood trusses form a mesmerizing diamond pattern on the ceiling, which rises like a bubble to its highest point in the center of the gym. The ceiling—as well as the outside of the structure and the bleachers and interior walls—is painted white, giving it the feel of a mini Metrodome, the former home of the Minnesota Twins.

"There's definitely a uniqueness to it," said Terry Byers, a 1964 Pine Village graduate. "It's little, but it's a classic place."

It was the home of the Pine Village Pine Knots until 1973, when the school was absorbed into Seeger. With consolidation on the horizon in '72, the Pine Knots gave the tiny Warren County community a reason to puff its chest, winning their first sectional in thirty-one years. It was a big, talented and high-scoring team, led by six-foot-five junior Bax Brutus. Pine Village upset Seeger 76–72 in the semifinals of the Fountain Central Sectional and then ousted North Vermillion 76–68 for the championship.

The Pine Knots—the smallest school to win a sectional that season—lost 71–69 to much larger Benton Central in the regional. It was the final game for Brutus, who was killed after the season when he was electrocuted in a farm accident.

"It was a once-in-a-lifetime type team for a school that size," said Bill Barrett, who coached four seasons at Pine Village. "We averaged eighty-three points that season. It was a smart team that knew how to play together."

The Pine Knots set the school record for points in a 118–78 home win over Fountain Central that season.

"We had 101 or 102 points with about four minutes left, and my assistant coach said we should put the starters back in to get the record," Barrett said. "I said, 'I hate to do that, I don't want to run it up.' But we did. Their coach [Jim Robinson] wasn't too happy with that. We won the sectional that year, but his team won it the next year. So it's all forgiven. We golf together now."

The Pine Village gym—which sits by itself behind the school off State Highway 26 on the east edge of town—is still used regularly for elementary school games and physical education classes. But with a population of just 250 people and districts all over the state facing budget cuts, the future of the school, and the gym, is in doubt.

On a crisp February afternoon, with the sun shining through the windows onto the wood floor, the seventy-year-old gym looks almost brand new.

"The floor wasn't too long, and the rims were soft," Barrett said. "That's why everybody loved to play there."

The Pine Village Pine Knots won a sectional in 1972, a year before the school was consolidated.

The Pine Village gym in Warren County west of Lafayette was built in 1940.

The elementary school, located about one hundred feet north of the gym, uses the gym for classes and basketball games.

WHEATLAND

For most communities in Indiana, the basketball boom didn't take hold until the 1920s. It was in that decade when large gymnasiums sprang up all over the state, at hotbeds like Martinsville, Washington and Vincennes.

Before the '20s and '30s, high school teams had to make do with the space available. Some played in dingy basements in the bowels of the school. Others played in makeshift barns. Still others braved the elements and played outdoors. At Wheatland, the teams in the early 1900s played outdoors or in a long hall inside the school. When a new school was built in 1908, it didn't include a court, and games were moved to a livery stable. In 1913, the team found a home on the second floor of Hedrick's Drugstore, owned by Willard Hedrick.

Wheatland's teams—which became known as the Jeeps in the 1930s but were then known as the "Reds" or "Harvesters"—used the large upstairs room for home games until a new school and gym were built in 1926. Hedrick's was a staple of life in Wheatland. The downstairs, with an ice cream parlor and soda fountain, was a gathering spot.

Bill Powell, a local man who bought the building from the town in 2004 (it was used as fire station), opened Small Town Crossing, a convenience store, on the lower level in 2008. In an adjoining room is a museum with pictures and artifacts of Wheatland's history.

Around back, on the southwest corner of the brick building, is a stairway that leads to the upstairs room. At the top of the stairs is a ticket booth. It's a large room with high ceilings, though hardly sufficient, it would appear, for a basketball game. On the south side, near midcourt, is a metal base where a potbellied stove once heated the room. On the other side are four wooden chairs that patrons once used to watch basketball games or movies, which were projected onto a screen that covered the stage on the east end of the room. A basketball hoop hangs from the west end with white lines painted on the floor for a half-court game by the Steen Township firemen.

"It had to have been hot up here when they played," Powell said. "The windows [on the north and south sides] would raise up, though."

Powell, a 1958 Wheatland graduate, said he spent $8,000 on a new roof, but

Above: The old hardware store was used as a fire station for several years. Bill Powell bought the building in 2004.

Left: This is the ticket booth located at the top of the stairs at the old Wheatland gym.

Opposite, inset: An exterior look at the former Hedrick's Drugstore. The gym was on the second floor.

it still leaks in the middle of the room. He intends to get the room cleaned up and back into condition where it can be used again. Wheatland consolidated into South Knox in 1967, and the school was razed a year later.

"I used to come up here when I was a kid," Powell said. "They'd have bingo, and they'd have church services. It's a nice big room."

At one time, it was even big enough for basketball.

MONROE CITY

Sam Alford grew up just eleven miles away in Washington but had not set foot in Monroe City until he interviewed for the basketball coaching job in 1966 at age twenty-four.

It was a one-year proposition: Monroe City was headed for consolidation the next year with neighboring Decker, Fritchton and Wheatland to form South Knox. The coaching job at South Knox had been promised to Decker coach Tom Richener. But Monroe City, led by Tim Sutton and Steve Like, won twenty consecutive games and made it to the championship of the Vincennes Sectional before losing to the host school.

That season launched Alford's coaching career. The school board tapped him for the South Knox job instead of Richener, and he stayed for four years. He then went to Martinsville for four seasons and to New Castle for the next twenty years. At New Castle, he won three hundred games and coached his son Steve, Indiana's Mr. Basketball, in 1983.

"It was a great way to start my coaching career," Sam Alford said of Monroe City. "The people were very basketball-minded and savvy. Growing up around there, I knew it would be a great basketball job, and it was even better than I thought."

The early teams at Monroe City played their games above a since-demolished livery stable located downtown in the Knox County community. A new gym was built in 1936 and attached to the west end of the school, which was constructed in 1910.

There were seven rows of wood bleachers on both sides of the court and a stage on one end.

The Monroe Central Blue Jeans were named for former Indiana governor James "Blue Jeans Bill" Williams, who grew up in rural Knox County and was known for wearing denim suits. He died in 1880 and is buried at the Walnut Grove cemetery outside of Monroe City.

The Blue Jeans usually ran into much larger Vincennes Lincoln in the sectional but did manage to win sectionals in 1949, '53 and '61. The '49 team lost to eventual state champion Jasper in the regional championship, 57–55.

"Bill Sutton was the superstar of that team," said Gerald Shouse, a six-foot-three senior center on the '53 sectional championship team. "They won the Wabash Valley Tournament, which was a really big deal back then. That was a really good team."

After the high school left in '67, the school continued as an elementary until 1999. The building is now used as the Blue Jeans Community Center, and the gym hosts flea

markets, community dinners, dog shows and home school basketball and volleyball games. The original scorer's table remains at midcourt on the west side. A trophy case in a hallway outside the gym honors the memories of past Monroe City teams.

One of the most memorable games in the gym was Monroe City's 6–0 win over Princeton in 1952.

"I tipped the ball to one of my teammates on the opening tip. He missed the shot, and I tipped it back in," Shouse said. "I was the leading scorer for the game with two points. They held the ball the whole game, and we let them do it. Then we gave them a taste of their own medicine in the fourth quarter and held it. We made four free throws and that was it."

Above: The Monroe City Blue Jeans played in a livery stable before this gym was built. Sam Alford's first coaching job was in Monroe City.

Opposite, inset: An exterior look at the 1936 Monroe City gym. It's now used as a community center. It was an elementary school until 1999.

BUTLER

It was a packed house at Eastside High School's game against Hicksville, Ohio, on January 24, 1987. Bobby Plump and Ray Craft of the famed 1954 Milan state championship team even made the trip. It wasn't the game itself that the standing-room-only crowd came to see; it was the venue.

The game was played at the 1936 Butler gym, which was last used as a high school gym until the late 1960s. Butler became Eastside in 1963, when it consolidated with Riverdale. On that night, the 1966 Eastside sectional championship team was honored.

"You could hardly walk in the gym," said Bob Gerber, who played on the '66 team. "It was like it was when we played, when people would be lined up outside the gym at three or four in the afternoon."

The former home of the Butler Windmills has survived relatively undisturbed for forty years since the high school moved out. It's been used for junior high games, softball practices and as a quasi community center. Though there has been some talk of tearing it down, it has survived the wrecking ball.

"I think people enjoy seeing it there," said Dick Obendorf, a 1953 Butler graduate. "It gives you some appreciation of what we had and probably don't have now. We lost some of that community loyalty after consolidation."

Large photos of the 1953 and '54 DeKalb County championship teams hang from the west wall of the gym, just to the right of the stage.

"We had a bunch of guys who had played together since sixth grade," Obendorf said. "We had a new coach, George Cherry, who wanted to run all the time. His philosophy was that a good offense was the best defense. He wanted us to shoot sixty or seventy times a game so we were running up and down the court quite a bit."

The gym features a brick interior with several rows of permanent bleachers on both sides. There is a five-foot brick wall on the north side and an unusual cutout area behind the east basket with several rows of bleachers behind it. The Eastside pep band would sit there during games in the 1960s.

The gym was featured in a commercial by a Fort Wayne television station.

"They've talked about getting rid of it because of the upkeep, but I hope not," said Gerber, who coached the junior varsity teams for sixteen years. "It's a solid steel structure, so it's not like it's going to fall in around itself. Hopefully we can keep using it for a long time."

An interior look at the Butler gym. It is used for junior high games and softball practices by Eastside High School, located in Butler.

This was the home of the Butler Windmills beginning in 1936.

Opposite, inset: An exterior look at the Butler gym in Dekalb County.

BLOOMFIELD

It was a short trip, but the walk from the Bloomfield school to the gym in the winter was an awfully cold one.

"It was just a little walkway, but it wasn't covered," said Marcus "Red" Oliphant, a 1945 Bloomfield graduate. "There'd be snow on the ground, and we'd run through there in the freezing cold because we didn't have dressing rooms in the gym."

Built in 1927 as a standalone structure to the east of the school, the gym also lacked a heating system. Hot air was piped in from the school. But keeping the gym warm never seemed to be problem. With a balcony that wrapped around all four sides, the fans were right on top of the action.

"Those old backboards were right up there next to the balcony," said Rex Hudson, who played in the gym as a 1949 Solsberry graduate and later was an assistant at Bloomfield for seventeen years. "You could reach right down there and swat the ball off the basket if you wanted to. Spencer came down with a really good team one year in the late '50s with a bunch of people and hung their banner right from the railing of the balcony."

Bloomfield had remarkable success for a school of its size, winning sectionals six times from 1928 to 1940. A tornado blew the roof off the gym in the 1930s, but it was quickly replaced.

Bloomfield's most successful run came under the watch of coach Guy Glover, who won 489 games from 1954 to 1977. The Cardinals won regional championships in '61 and '65 in the state's former one-class format. An oversized photo of each team hangs on the north and south walls of the gym, which is now used as an auxiliary gym for practices and physical education classes.

"It was a heck of a lot bigger than some of the gyms we played in," Oliphant said. "At Scotland [which consolidated into Bloomfield in 1955], you would just bang right into the wall when you went up for a shot. At least we had mats up."

In the late 1950s, a crow's-nest was built in the southeast corner of the gym for the scorer's table. A player would have to come around from the other side of the court and yell up to the table to check in. The running joke was that the hometown official scorer didn't necessarily have to look down, especially when Larry Bird from Springs Valley attempted to check in.

For many years, music director Ari "Cub" Laughlin led the band, which sat on the south end of the gym. Laughlin also doubled as the custodian.

The gym was last used by the high school in 1985, when the new gym—named for Glover—was built. The school was built around the old facility, making it difficult to tell from the outside that it remains.

The 1927 Bloomfield gym at one time had a balcony all the way around. The Bloomfield school has been built around it.

A photo of the 1961 regional championship team hangs at one end of the gym. Guy Glover coached at Bloomfield from 1954 to 1977.

An exterior look at the Bloomfield school in Greene County. The old gym is in the middle of the building and is used for physical education classes.

WASHINGTON

Chuck Harmon and Jim Riffey grew up in the same neighborhood on the west side of Washington. Together they would form a nearly unstoppable combination that dominated opponents for two seasons in the early 1940s.

"We were like brothers," said Harmon, who became the first black American to play for the Cincinnati Reds in 1954. "We told all the guys from the south side of town that we never would have won state if it wasn't for the guys from the west end."

Washington won state championships in 1941 and '42, combining for a 57-6 record those two seasons. The Washington gym, built in 1925 after the team and community outgrew the basement gym at the 1913 schoolhouse, was a happening place.

The Hatchets—which became the team's official nickname the same year the new gym opened—won their first state championship in 1930, filling the gym for every home game. (Though the capacity was listed at fifty-two hundred in 1920's Washington yearbook, it is believed that meant to include on-floor seating for events like graduations and plays; the actual capacity was closer to thirty-six hundred, although four thousand people regularly packed the seats.)

The crowd noise—and sometimes loose change flung in the direction of the referees—literally descended onto the court. The layout featured eight rows of bleacher seats, starting twelve feet off the floor, all the way around the gym. On the floor level, there were chair-back seats with a few rows of bleachers below.

"When they'd have sectionals, they didn't have reserved seating and would just sell tickets until you couldn't get anybody else in the gymnasium," said John Helm, a 1965 graduate. "They would sit in the aisles, even for regular season games. It was a very dangerous situation from a fire marshal's perspective. When they sold all the seats, they would congregate probably twenty feet deep in the doorways."

The gym was used until the 1965–66 season, when the "Hatchet House"—an impressive structure with a capacity of more than seven thousand fans—was built just a few yards away. The old gym is currently used as a junior high gym. In the mid-1970s, in between the time he dropped out of Indiana University and enrolled at Indiana State, Larry Bird played in a YMCA league at the old Washington gym.

Helm said "it felt like the roof was coming off the gym" when something good would happen for the home team. For the sectional, which included twelve or thirteen teams in the 1950s, fans would fill the gym an hour before the game.

"It was like the gold rush when they opened the doors," he said. "It's hard to describe. From a player's perspective it was much more enjoyable in a smaller gym than a huge one. The Hatchet House is so vast and huge that you lost that personalization. Bigger isn't always better. The place would explode."

For Riffey and Harmon, both eighty-six, the gym represents the best times of their lives. Riffey, a six-foot-five center who went on to a standout college career at Tulane and played briefly in the NBA, remembers his mother cheering from the bleachers after he would score.

Almost seventy years later, the images are still burned in his memory.

"I'll bet if you walked in there at night," Riffey said, "you could hear the whispers."

An exterior look at the former Washington gym. It was built in 1925.

The Washington gym was built in 1925, when the community outgrew the basement gym at the 1913 schoolhouse.

VINCENNES LINCOLN

Ralph Holscher doesn't hesitate when asked what he remembers most about Adams Coliseum. "Too many losses," the former Vincennes Rivet coach says with a laugh.

Vincennes Lincoln was truly dominant in the sixty-two seasons it called the Adams Coliseum home. From 1926 to 1988, the Alices won more than six hundred games in the gym and an astounding fifty sectional championships. Vincennes also won the regional at home in 1929, '39 and '52. Huntingburg later wrested the regional away from Vincennes in the 1950s.

Adams Coliseum was built at a cost of $106,955. The popularity of the team, buoyed by a state championship in 1923, necessitated a new venue. Beginning in 1917, the Alices (then known as the Pirates) played in the basement of what is now an administrative building, next door to Adams Coliseum.

Even now, the facility seems enormous. Adams Coliseum is built into the city block at the corner of Buntin and Seventh Streets like an old-time baseball stadium. Except for a small parking lot across Buntin to the west, the only available parking is along the city streets.

"There was nowhere to park," said Holscher, who graduated from the small Knox County school of Oaktown in 1945 and played in sectional games at Adams Coliseum. "You had to park all over town. People would park in front of other people's houses."

The capacity listed inside the coliseum is 4,838. When it was originally built, there was no seating at floor level; rollaway bleachers on both sides were added later. Above an eight-foot brick wall all the way around the court are eleven rows of bleachers seats. Beneath the bleachers on two sides are four rows of chair-back seats.

"The first time I went to a game there was 1951, and I was in the second grade," said Hugh Schaefer, who grew up twenty miles northeast of Vincennes in Freelandville. "It was the biggest place I'd seen in my life. I remember coming out of the dressing room on one end when we played there in sectionals. It looked like it was ten miles to the other end of the floor. I'll never forget that. It had a great mystique to it."

Because Vincennes Lincoln dominated sectionals for so many years, the smaller county schools were conditioned to despise the Alices. On the rare occasion that another school won the sectional—like Decker winning title games over Vincennes in 1943 and '44—it was reason to celebrate.

"They were the hated team," Schaefer said. "I've never worn anything green [Vincennes' predominant color] in my life. I've never bought a green car."

But even the dislike for the Alices doesn't diminish the memories of Adams Coliseum. The future of the building was in doubt as of the spring of 2010. Clark Middle School used the gym for games after a new high school was built, but the construction of a new middle school for the 2010–11 school year means Adams Coliseum will sit empty.

"You hope there's enough sentiment there to do something with it," Holscher said.

The Adams Coliseum in Vincennes has been used by Clark Middle School for several years, but the opening of a new middle school means it may sit empty.

The Adams Coliseum in Vincennes, built in 1926, was one of the early classic venues in Indiana high school basketball. Vincennes Lincoln won the state campionship in 1923, a coup that hastened the construction of Adams Coliseum.

WARREN

It was a good idea, it seemed, when the gym was built in 1926—a skylight that would allow the sun to shine in through the roof during the day and the moonlight at night. It was basketball under the stars.

There was just one problem with that idea. When the Warren gym was packed with people, as it usually was on Friday nights in the winter, condensation would build up on the glass windows, and water would drip from the ceiling. It got to the point where referees learned to carry a rag in their back pockets to wipe the moisture from the floor.

"That thing would sweat like crazy," said Keith Spahr, a 1957 graduate who also coached at the school from 1961 to 1965. "You wouldn't be able to play very long and they'd have to mop the floor. It was that way the majority of the time."

The skylight has since been covered, both saving the gym floor and helping to cut back on heating expenses. The Warren Lightning Five—named by a sportswriter, who wrote that the team was "fast as lightning" in a win over Marion early in the 1900s—last played on the court in the 1965–66 season before consolidating into Huntington North with all the rest of the Huntington County schools.

The school continued as an elementary until 1982. The next year it was turned into a community center with the aid of a substantial financial gift from 1922 graduate Clifford Knight, who owned an air conditioning business in Michigan. Years later, George Bergman also left a portion of his estate for the operating expenses of the building, and it was renamed the Knight-Bergman Center.

Except for a year and a half in the early 1990s, when it was converted back to an elementary for Southern Wells after its school burned down, it has been a community center. The gym is used for youth leagues and pickup games six or seven days a week.

"It's an old building and takes a lot of upkeep, but it's really doing great," said Bob Pond, a 1947 Warren graduate. "Community groups use the large room, which used to be a study hall room, and there's alumni events there all the time."

The bleachers in the gym were donated by the class of 1928. There is a stage on the west end with large wooden doors and a lightning bolt with the number "5" painted on the court. Warren never won a sectional and won its only county tournament in 1960.

The old school is maintained by volunteers, though a fundraising effort that had raised roughly $60,000 through the spring of 2010 could be used to pay for part-time help.

"It's somewhat of a struggle since all the work is done by volunteers, but it means a lot to the community," said Jim Howell, a 1960 graduate. "Rather than tear the building down like a lot of towns have, we've gotten quite a bit out of it."

The Warren gym was built in 1926 and was used by elementary students until 1982.

The former Warren school is now thriving as the Knight-Bergman Center, a community center in the Huntington County town.

Warren's basketball teams had one of the unique Indiana high school nicknames: the Lightning Five.

OWENSVILLE

It's a neat-looking building: dark brick with "Owensville Kickapoos" painted to the left of the front doors. A row of bushes nearby is perfectly manicured, and the grass is freshly cut. The state flag of Indiana and the United States flag fly proudly above the front walk.

But it's not the outside of the Owensville gym that makes an impression. Thanks to an alumni base with an appreciation for basketball history, the gym has become a living museum of sorts.

"We're awfully proud of it," said Ken Sharp, a former teacher and coach who led the charge to save the gym from demolition after the adjoining school was demolished in 1992.

The gym was built in 1950 and was the first underground gym in Indiana. Underground gyms became a unique style in the '50s. Owensville also has the distinction of having the first glass backboards, installed by coach and principal Harry Champ before the sectional in 1921. One of the backboards hangs from a wall on the west end of the gym; the other is at the Indiana Basketball Hall of Fame in New Castle.

Along the wall of the concourse that rings the perimeter of the gym are newspaper articles, letter jackets, class photos, trophies and other assorted artifacts donated by alumni. On the west wall is the original scoreboard from the old gym, which was located inside the 1916 school. Owensville had a high school until 1974, when it consolidated to form Gibson Southern with neighboring Fort Branch and Haubstadt. When a new elementary school was built in 1992, the town and park board bought the gym and renamed it the REH Center, which stands for Recreational, Educational and Historical.

Sharp, who was the varsity coach from 1965 to 1968, organized the alumni to raise money to save the gym. It's now used for youth basketball, adult leagues, senior walking and rentals. The Gibson Southern girls' basketball team played a throwback game in the gym in 2008.

"We put a new roof on it when we first got it and put a new boiler in it," Sharp said. "We had the floor refinished and painted the walls and bleachers. Most of the work is done by volunteers."

The outside walls of the gym were originally made of glass. Don Barrett, the president of the REH board, said he remembered a car sliding on the ice, right through the glass and into the gym. The walls were later replaced with concrete.

"I remember we'd have tournaments in here during the day, and the sun would almost blind you," Sharp said.

Owensville hosted sectionals the first three years the gym was open and won the 1953 sectional on its home court. The team is gone, but the gym is very much alive.

"People would stand up here," said Sharp, leaning on a railing overlooking the floor on the east end. "We had signs not to stand on the railing, but that's what everybody would do. You got a lot of help coaching from the guys up here."

All the way around the perimeter of the Owensville gym are artifacts that honor the history of the Owensville Kickapoos. The Gibson Southern girls' team played a game there in 2008.

An exterior look at the 1950 Owensville gym.

The Owensville gym was built in 1950 and touched off a new style of gym, as it was built underground.

ALFORDSVILLE

To find Alfordsville, you have to be looking for it.

"It's not on the way to anywhere," said Kenneth Bussell, an Alfordsville native.

There isn't much to the Daviess County community anymore. There was once a grocery store, a convenience store, a restaurant, a hardware store and everything else needed to sustain a little town.

"It was a bustling little community at one time," Bussell said.

Not so much now. Barely one hundred people live in town, which has no businesses to speak of. One of the biggest buildings in town—as of April 2010—is the former basketball home of the Alfordsville Yellow Jackets.

It's falling apart. Windows are broken out, and the roof is rotting. It has been privately owned since the 1970s, but the town hoped in the spring of 2010 that it would be able to buy the building and tear it down.

The gym was built in 1953 and was attached to the school, which was located on what is now an empty lot north of the building. The gym had several classrooms, bleachers on both sides and a stage on the east end. There were stairways on the northeast and southeast corners that led up the classrooms and a common area where fans could watch the game behind the basket on the east end.

Prior to 1953, Alfordsville did not have a gym of its own.

"We would rent the Loogootee gym and play our home games there," said Marlin Kelso, a 1950 graduate.

The Yellow Jackets once practiced outdoors, where the gym was later built.

"We didn't know any different," Kelso said. "It was cinders. It was a big deal to us when they poured concrete."

The last graduating class at Alfordsville in 1965 had nine students. The school consolidated into Barr-Reeve with Barr Township the following year. Bussell was a sophomore when the school closed, and he graduated from Barr-Reeve in 1967.

"We had five players on our junior varsity team my sophomore year," Bussell said. "I was pretty rough and would foul out of a lot of games. So we'd end up with four players, and the other team would take a guy out and they'd play four-on-four."

The town hopes to eventually use the property for its fire department.

"It's an eyesore," Kelso said. "Hopefully we can get it torn down soon."

Above: The Alfordsville Yellow Jackets only used this gym for twelve years. The school consolidated into Barr-Reeve in 1965.

Opposite, inset: The 1953 Alfordsville gym in Daviess County is falling apart and will likely be torn down soon. The teams practiced on a concrete slab outside before the gym was built.

WINSLOW

One of Indiana's great high school nicknames—the Winslow Eskimos—originated because of an old, cold gym.

Winslow didn't have a gym until 1922, when the "Cow Barn" was built at a cost of around $8,000. The gym, which looked a bit like a barn from the outside, had limited seating. Fans would pack the stage on one end, fill the balconies on each side and stand along the perimeter of the court. The building was heated by four potbellied stoves, but it was generally a drafty and cold place to watch a game in the winter.

As a result, the Winslow Champions became the Winslow Eskimos in the 1930s.

"That building was cold as ice most of the time," said John Dedman, a 1954 Winslow graduate.

The Cow Barn was where the legendary Richard "Dick" Farley played his home games, at least until the building was condemned in 1949. Farley led Winslow to a 20-0 record as a junior in 1949 before the Eskimos were defeated by eventual state champion Jasper in the sectional. A year later, Winslow won a regional for the first time.

Farley went on to a standout career at Indiana, where he started for Branch McCracken's 1953 NCAA champions. After playing in the NBA for the Syracuse Nationals and Detroit Pistons, Farley died in 1969 at age thirty-seven.

"Dick Farley is the most underrated basketball player Indiana University has ever had," McCracken told the *Evansville Courier & Press* in 1972. "He was one of the

greatest defensive players to ever play in the Big Ten."

Carroll Edrington played as a junior on the 1954 team that also won a regional championship.

"We had a really good team and everybody was considered about equal," Edrington said. "But Farley, he was the best thing to ever come out of Pike County. He was a gentleman, too."

Winslow continued to practice in the Cow Barn and play some of its home games eight miles away at Oakland City College until a new $107,000 gym was dedicated on November 6, 1951. The new gym featured bleacher seating on three sides and a stage on one end with a capacity of fifteen hundred.

The Eskimos used the gym until 1974, when it was consolidated into Pike Central. The adjacent two-story school was torn down soon after, and a new elementary school was built to the west of the gym.

The gym was restored in 1999 after a lightning strike tore a hole through the roof. The original wood floor has been replaced

Above: The Winslow gym is now used for various community events. It was renovated in 1999, although it looks much the same as when it was built.

Opposite, inset: An exterior look at the Winslow gym in Pike County. It was dedicated in 1951. The Winslow Eskimos played in a building called the Cow Barn until it was condemned in 1949.

by rubber surface. There is an old scoreboard on the north end and a sign proclaiming it the "Kern McGlothlin Gymnasium" in honor of the man who coached the Eskimos for ten seasons in the glory years of the '40s and '50s.

"Winslow had some terrific basketball teams," said Maurice Thompson, a 1952 graduate. "My dad played back in the '20s, and they had really good teams then."

The Winslow graduates would get together every three years for an alumni game at the gym, though that tradition ended in 2006.

"We all got too old," Thompson said.

OTWELL

The Otwell Millers were a popular basketball team in the 1960s. So popular, in fact, that the home games had to be moved to neighboring Petersburg for the last eight years of the school's existence.

"We wanted to keep having a game a year there," said Howard "Andy" Anderson, who coached at Otwell from 1960 to 1974. "I'll never forget, we had a game against Prairie Heights when Joe LaGrange was the coach there. The Prairie Heights people couldn't get in the gym it was so packed. I went around and got the principal and his wife in the building. That pretty well convinced everyone we couldn't play games there anymore."

The gym was built in 1941 as a Work Projects Administration project. The brick building has five rows of bleachers on each side and a stage on the east end opposite the main doors.

"Otwell didn't have a home gym before then," said Donald Barrett, a 1948 graduate. "They would play other places, like Winslow or Ireland. Some high schools back then would just play outside in the dirt."

After Otwell was consolidated into Pike Central with Petersburg and Winslow in 1974, the school was torn down and the gym left standing. Pike County owns the building, but it's leased to the local Ruritan Club for one dollar a year. A large kitchen and dining room are attached to the north side of the gym and used when the building hosts various community events, including the Little Miss Firecracker contest every fourth of July.

A community library was recently built on the northeast side of the building at a cost of $112,000. The inside of the gym looks much like when it was originally constructed, except for white siding covering the inside instead of brick. The floor is the original from 1941.

"It's available for rent, and we have quite a few flea markets in there," said Roger Knight, a former teacher at the school who helps operate the building. "It gets quite a bit of use."

Though Anderson's teams rarely played games in the gym, they practiced in it "every day except Sunday." The best of his teams was the 1969 group that won the program's only sectional. Steve Barrett, Donald Barrett's son, was a junior on that team and later played four years at Murray State. The Millers knocked off host Washington in the first round of the sectional and then defeated Barr-Reeve and North Daviess to claim the title. Unbeaten Vincennes finally ousted Otwell in the regional.

"People around here really took to that team," Anderson said.

Above: The Otwell gym in Pike County was built as a Work Projects Administration project in 1941. It now hosts various community events.

Opposite, inset: An exterior look at the 1941 Otwell gym. The Millers played here until consolidation in 1974, although home games in later years were moved to Petersburg.

FAIRBANKS

In 1990, with an enrollment of just eighty-five students in kindergarten through eighth grade, the school at Fairbanks closed its doors. If the Northeast Sullivan Community School Corporation had the $85,000 it would have cost to tear the building down, there would probably be nothing more than a grass field on the west side of town now.

But the school, built in 1910, and the gym, added on to the south side fifteen years later, remains a vibrant part of the peaceful, unincorporated community tucked away near the Illinois border in northwest Sullivan County.

The school sat empty and rotting away until 1994, when the school corporation tuned it over to a group of community members—led by Wanda Chambers—called Growth in Fairbanks Township. Volunteers donated time and money to turn the building, and especially the gym, into a community center. Later, a group called Life in Fairbanks Township formed, and in 2007, the organization was awarded a $500,000 grant from the Office of Rural and Community Affairs with the stipulation that the building would stay open for five years.

Among the upgrades was a new gym floor. The gym features a balcony on the north side and east and west ends and a stage on the south side. It was used by the high school team the Fairbanks Trojans until the school was consolidated with Farmersburg, Shelburn and Hymera to form North Central in 1957.

"People would sit up in the balcony or stand against the rail," said Dean Power, class of 1947. "But they wouldn't allow anyone to stand behind the backboard so they couldn't knock the ball out or put it in."

Before the gym was added on to the school in 1925, the Fairbanks teams played in a makeshift gym above Pound and Co., a grocery store in the middle of town. The building was torn down more than a decade ago.

"It wasn't too bad," Wayne Dix, also a 1947 graduate, said of the original gym. "The ceiling was a little low. Things have obviously changed dramatically since those days."

Norman Drake, a 1937 graduate, said he wasn't much for basketball but played anyway. There were only eleven people in his class, a typical size at Fairbanks.

"We pretty well had to play," Drake said. "There were just a few of us. There wouldn't have been enough to have a team."

One of the more popular events was the annual tournament when the Fairbanks classes—freshmen, sophomores, juniors

Above: The Fairbanks gym in Sullivan County has survived as a community center. Before this gym opened, the Fairbanks teams played in a gym above a grocery store in the middle of town.

Opposite, inset: In 1925, the Fairbanks gym was built behind the 1910 school.

and seniors—played against one another. The 1946 class, which had just four students, had to borrow from another class to play.

The grant has helped the financial situation of the Fairbanks school for now, but it will take a continued effort from volunteers to keep it going.

Chambers died in 2005. Though she didn't attend Fairbanks, her husband, Nib Chambers, and five children did. Her obituary read: "The last few years her dream had been to restore the old Fairbanks School to be used as a restaurant, youth center and community building. May her dream become a reality!"

"It was her baby," said daughter Vickie McCullough, who lives just east of the school. "She put so much time and effort into it. It really meant a lot to her."

GRAYSVILLE

With seating for 360 people, the Graysville gym is hardly luxurious. But it compared favorably to many of the other cracker boxes in Sullivan County.

"Pimento, Merom, New Lebanon, Pleasantville—they were all smaller gyms," said Bill Cox, a 1950 graduate who has lived in Graysville his entire life. "We had one of the nicest playing areas in the county. Sullivan's was big, but ours was just as nice."

In 1915, a modern brick schoolhouse was built just to the west of the two-story brick school that Graysville had outgrown since its construction in 1903. The 1915 school featured a gym/auditorium that ran north and south. But that school burned down near the end of the 1927 school year.

In a few short months, a new building was constructed on the same site at a cost of $90,000 (senior boys worked with the contractors). School started late in the fall of 1927, and students went to school six days a week to make up for lost time. The gym was also built in the same spot, though this time it was larger and ran east to west. It included a balcony on three sides with three rows of seats, three rows of seats on the floor level on the north and south sides and a stage on the west end.

Building a larger gym proved wise. The Graysville Greyhounds won a sectional championship in 1929 and typically packed the gym until the school was absorbed by Sullivan in 1961. Fewer than one hundred

yards north of the school is a building that has been used for a variety of purposes, including a dance hall. In later years, people would gather there after basketball games to celebrate, mourn or complain.

The Graysville school continued as an elementary until 2003, when students were shipped to Sullivan.

"It was a four-star school," said Susie Pierce, a third-generation Graysville resident. "For a long lineage of people the school was the center of the town. To see it go would have been the deterioration of the community."

A group of community members called the Truman Township Youth Foundation took control of the building, with the idea of converting it into a community center. A year after the elementary moved out, the Rural Community Academy, a charter school funded by Ball State, moved in. The township recently received a grant for $40,000 over the next five years. Among

the renovations will be a new gym floor. The original hardwood was replaced by a cork floor in the early 1970s.

Graysville has gotten its money's worth from the eighty-three-year-old building.

"They were going to board it up, but the community got together and got the ball rolling again," Cox said. "Everybody does their part to pitch in and make it work."

Above: A look down from the balcony of the 1927 Graysville gym. A charter school now uses the gym and the adjoining school. The Graysville Greyhounds played here until the school was absorbed by Sullivan in 1961.

Opposite, inset: An exterior look at the Graysville school in Sullivan County.

MOORESVILLE

Jim Harvey twisted his ankle two minutes into the final home game of the 1957–58 and took a seat on the bench. He enjoyed the show from the Mooresville bench for the rest of the night.

Bill Altman, a six-foot-three center who went on to play for Branch McCracken at Indiana, scored a school-record fifty-four points in Mooresville's season-ending win over Danville.

"I had something like twenty-two points at halftime," said Altman, who now lives in Las Vegas. "We had a reasonably good lead, and the two other seniors, Bill Swinney and Wendell Boyd, said we ought to go for the record. Our coach [Glen Sparks] was emphatic that a win was a win. But in the second half, I'd get a rebound and throw it out, and my teammates would wait for me. By that time, the Danville teams had pretty well given up. So I think part of it was that they gave me some gift points."

More than fifty years later, Altman's record still stands. Mooresville played one more season in the gym where he set the record before a new school and gym were built for the 1959–60 school year.

The Mooresville gym—or Newby Gym, as it was later known, named for local businessman and philanthropist Arthur Newby, one of the founding fathers of the Indianapolis Motor Speedway—was constructed in the fall of 1920 and dedicated on New Year's Eve. The festivities that night included a concert by the Friends Church orchestra, a tug of war between

area youth and four basketball games: the Mooresville boys against Center Grove; the Mooresville girls against Brownsburg; the Monrovia girls against Center Grove; and a Mooresville alumni team against the Mooresville Elks Club.

The gym was constructed at a cost of $23,000. All of the families that helped donate money were given free passes to basketball games for one year.

Brian Wiser, a Mooresville native who has researched the building's history extensively, said that John Wooden never played in the gym. Wooden played at Martinsville in the 1920s, but the neighboring towns did not play during that time.

"Mooresville and Martinsville apparently disliked each other so much that they wouldn't play," Wiser said. "I had always assumed he did."

The Newby Gym was the first built in Morgan County specifically for basketball. Portable chairs were used in the balcony on the east end, above the front doors; on the west end was a stage. On the north and

Above: The Mooresville gym retains a classic feel and has been utilized by junior basketball leagues for several years.

Opposite, inset: The Mooresville gym was dedicated on New Year's Eve 1920. It hosted sectionals in 1922 and '23.

south sides were several rows of bleachers. Despite its relatively small size (about five hundred capacity), the Newby Gym hosted sectionals in 1922 and '23. Martinsville took the sectional back when it built its fifty-two-hundred-capacity gym in 1924.

The junior high used the gym until 1965, and the elementary school used it for physical education classes until 1993. That same year, the Mooresville Junior Basketball League signed a lease with the school corporation for sole use and upkeep of the facility. In 1996, a "Save the Newby Gym" committee formed to raise money to repair the building. A grant from the Lilly Endowment in the amount of $77,150 was presented to the committee in 1997 and helped pay for renovations that included a new gym floor.

Today, the gym is used regularly by the junior basketball leagues and for alumni events.

"What you remember most is that it was, and still is, part of a beautiful campus," said Erma (Glidden) Holmes, a former cheerleader and 1958 graduate. "You can still picture everybody sitting around the campus, girls in those big skirts. It was a neat place."

KENTLAND

Like many communities in Indiana in the 1940s and '50s, Kentland had outgrown its gym. So with a population of 1,800, Kentland built a gymnasium in 1950 that seated 2,250.

"Typical Indiana," said Greg Logan, who grew up in Kentland and is now the town manager. "They built a gym bigger than the town."

Kentland had long outgrown its previous gym. Prior to the new construction, the Blue Devils played in the basement of the red brick school to the north, built in 1921. The only seating was on the stage and a balcony above the floor on one side.

Kentland hosted sectionals every year from 1958 to 1966, when the Newton County school five miles from the Illinois border was consolidated into South Newton with Brook and Goodland. The Blue Devils won their fifth and final sectional in '65, defeating rival Fowler 67–60 in the sectional championship. From 1953 to 1967, Fowler won ten sectionals.

"We had some really good athletes that year," said Logan, a sophomore on the '65 team. "Unfortunately, we would switch coaches every couple years. Fowler was the powerhouse, and they had the same coaches [Herschell Mallory and Dale Smith] for several years. We were always starting over."

Photos of Kentland's sectional championship teams hang in the lobby west of the gym, which is now a community center and hosts everything from the annual Oktoberfest to weddings and cage fighting. The school was used for several years as an elementary but was razed in 1996, when a new school was built north of Kentland.

The town received a $500,000 grant that year to put in new baseball fields where the school was once located. The gym was also refurbished with the town's money; improvements included a new roof and ceiling and a refinished floor.

The gym has eleven rows of bleachers running the length of the floor on the north and south sides, starting about four feet off the floor above a concrete wall. For sectional tournaments, temporary bleachers were added on the stage.

Though it still fills numerous roles, the Kentland gym had a relatively short lifespan as a high school gym.

"Only about fifteen years," Logan said. "It wasn't used very long at all."

Opposite, top: An exterior look at the Kentland gym in Newton County, built in 1950.

Opposite, bottom: The gym in Kentland hosted sectionals every year from 1958 to 1966. It's now a community center. The Kentland Blue Devils played in the basement of the 1921 school before it was built.

HEBRON

Hebron had one of the more modern gyms in the area when it was built as a Work Projects Administration project in 1939.

"We played a game early in my senior year at Washington Township and got beat," said Bernard Martin, a 1949 Hebron graduate. "Our coach [Dick Falls] really got on us for that. That place was a little cracker box. You could hardly move.

Hebron came back and beat Washington Township in the Porter County Tournament that year, defeating Morgan Township in the championship game at Valparaiso. The previous year, in '48, the Hawks had lost in the county finals to Portage in overtime.

"We were ahead of Portage by two with just a few seconds left, and they got fouled and sent a guy to the foul line," Martin remembered. "Everybody thought the referee said 'two shots.' Well, the guy missed the first free throw, and the Portage player standing right next to me grabbed the ball and put it in. I could have had it really easily, but everybody was just standing there. Then we had a couple guys foul out and lost in overtime. That was a tough one."

When it was built in 1939, Hebron's home gym ran north and south, with a balcony on the west side with four rows of bleachers; there were also bleachers underneath. On the east was a wall that butted up closely to the sideline. When the school was renovated in 1973, the east wall was knocked out, and the floor was lengthened to run east and west. A balcony was added to the east end and pullout bleachers to the north and south sides. The Hawks used that facility until a new school building was erected in 2005, with a 2,010-seat gymnasium.

The 1939 building, now used as part of the junior high, originally had an auditorium and classrooms to the west of the gym. That portion has since been razed. The gym is now used for junior high games, practices and physical education classes.

Opposite, top: An exterior look at the Hebron gym in Porter County.

Opposite, bottom: The Hebron gym in Porter County was built as a Work Projects Administration project in 1939. It was renovated in 1973 and used as the high school gym until 2005.

BROOK

It doesn't take long for Don Parrish, class of 1958, to announce the Brook Aces' claim to fame. "Most sectional championships in the county," Parrish says with pride.

Though Brook won't add to that record anytime soon, having consolidated with Kentland and Goodland into South Newton in 1966, the Aces do own a Newton County record twelve sectional titles. Four of those teams played their home games at the gym built in 1936 north of the 1903 schoolhouse. The town took ownership of the buildings in 1997 from the school corporation and tore the school down. The gym was remodeled, including a new roof and an additional room to the north where class photos hang from the walls.

The gym now serves a variety of functions as a community center. Four nights a week, it's opened for kids in town to play basketball.

"We rent it out for wedding receptions and things like that," Parrish said. "Girl scouts, boy scouts, cub scouts and dances. I'm just glad we have it."

Before the gym was built in 1936, the Brook Aces played in what was once an overall factory named Lewin & Son. In that building, built in 1907, women would sit near the windows along both sides at sewing machines. In the eight years the plant operated in Brook, it employed more than fifty women. It didn't sit vacant for long, as it became the Brook Community Center in 1916 and the basketball teams used it until 1934, when it was struck by lightning and burned to the ground.

Construction soon began on the new gym, which was named for longtime school board member T.E. Collier and attached to the school. There were—and still are—five rows of bleachers on both the north and south sides and a few rows on the north end. There is a stage on the east end, though the original purple curtain has been replaced. The capacity was approximately four hundred.

Brook won the sectional for the final time in 1953, defeating Morocco, Fair Oaks and DeMotte at Rensselaer. One of the school's top players came through a few years later. Tom Nelson, a slender, six-foot-three center, accumulated a school record of 1,442 points by the time he graduated in 1958. Coach Phil Miller, who started at Brook in 1952–53, believed the '58 team was his best, but it lost 49–47 in double overtime to Rensselaer in the sectional championship at Kentland.

"Nelson was a pretty big boy," said Larry Lyons, class of '57. "He was a giant back in our day. [Our teams] ran all the time. We weren't afraid if we were behind by twenty points because we'd just keep running."

Opposite, top: An exterior look at the Brook gym. It's used for a variety of functions.

Opposite, bottom: The Brook gym in Newton County was built in 1936. It's now a community center. The Brook Aces won a county record twelve sectional championships.

CULVER

Before Milan, there was Culver.

In 1944, the Culver Indians—with an enrollment of about one hundred at the time—won their first regional in school history. In the semistate at Hammond, Culver defeated Converse 26–17 in the first game before losing 24–23 to LaPorte in a game that would have advanced the Indians to the four-team state finals. LaPorte went on to lose 41–38 to eventual state champion Evansville Bosse.

"We had a really good chance to be the first Milan," said 1945 Culver graduate Ralph Pedersen, referring to the 1954 team that won the state championship and inspired the movie *Hoosiers*. "We were one of three undefeated teams in the state that year [28-1] before we lost to LaPorte. When we went down and watched the state finals, we knew we could have beaten Bosse."

Coach Paul Underwood had a tremendous sixteen-year run as coach, beginning right out of Franklin College in 1929. That was the same year Culver opened its new gymnasium, defeating Plymouth in the first game at the new facility, which was known as "the community center." Culver hosted sectionals several times in the 1930s, winning as the host team in 1936.

The gym had permanent bleachers on the east and west ends and the south side, above a short brick wall. There was a stage on the north side.

"Back in the '30s and '40s, it was probably the best gym in the county," Pedersen said.

Underwood achieved legendary status at Culver, winning seven county championships, five sectionals and two regionals in his sixteen years. After Culver, he coached for twenty-seven years at Goshen, where he also served as athletic director.

"He was a very unassuming coach," Pedersen said. "He'd set up the parameters and basic ideas, like a give and go or a back cut, and let you go play. Back then, coaches couldn't stand up during games. He wore out more pairs of pants than anybody."

Pedersen and Underwood are both members of the Indiana Basketball Hall of Fame. Pedersen went on to play at Tulane and then coached for two years at Tyner before returning to Culver and coaching for three years (1954–57). He was then hired as an assistant at Tulane and was the head coach for the Green Wave from 1964 to 1971.

Pedersen retired and returned to Culver in 1992. The gym where he once played and coached was recently renovated

Above: The Culver gym was recently renovated and is used for elementary school games and practices.

Opposite, inset: An exterior look at the 1929 Culver gym in Marshall County. The Culver Indians called this gym home when they made a sensational tournament run in 1944.

and reconstructed for $709,344. Locker rooms and bathrooms were added, and the permanent seating was torn out and replaced with retractable bleachers. The floor in the southeast corner also had to be raised about four inches.

"You could roll a ball down the middle of the court, and it would end up in the corner," Pedersen said with a laugh.

Pedersen still works as a volunteer coach with kids in second through sixth grades. The gym looks a bit different—and brighter—than it did when he played there, but it serves the same function.

"It's still a good gymnasium," he said. "It's not a field house or an arena, but it does the job and has for a long time."

MOROCCO

If it wasn't for a few proud Morocco alums, the school and gym in the center of the Newton County community could have been a decaying relic by 2010.

In 2006, the North Newton school board voted to consolidate the elementary schools at Morocco and Lake Village and build a new elementary school near the high school outside of town. But an alumni group, organized by 1957 graduate Bonnie Storey, organized a successful remonstrance, gathering the signatures from every township in the school corporation. Shortly thereafter, a new school board voted again. In May 2009, ground broke on a new wing for the elementary school. The old high school, which will house the administrative offices, is directly south of the new addition.

The gym, built in 1936, was at the heart of the alums' decision to fight the consolidation. At the time it was built, with a seating capacity of sixteen hundred for basketball games, it was the largest gym in Newton County. The style was similar to that of Lebanon's Memory Hall, with permanent seating on three sides and big windows above the last row of bleachers. Two concrete sidewalks led from College Avenue to the two corner entrances facing the north.

"From Calumet to Lafayette, it was the nicest gym in northwest Indiana," said John Kessler, who played on Morocco's 1956 sectional championship team.

Morocco's previous gym had been in the basement of the old school, called "the Pit." That area remains in the old school but has

since been redesigned as office space. After the new gym was built, Morocco hosted sectionals six times from 1937 to 1946. But it wasn't until '56 that the Beavers finally won their second sectional championship in school history, twenty-two years after the first.

Morocco defeated Rensselaer 65–58 in the sectional championship, which was played at Rensselaer.

"Coming out of town, heading back to Morocco, we had a caravan of about three of four cars and state policeman from Morocco leading us back home," Kessler said. "We were the last car. A town cop from Rensselaer pulls us over. He's in the process of writing us a ticket when the state officer from Morocco comes back with his siren on and chews the guy out. The Rensselaer cop was just mad we'd beaten his team."

Morocco also played six-man football and back then was better known as a football town. Lodes also coached the football team and went on to coach football at Monticello, Elwood and Connersville.

Above: The Morocco gym was built in 1936. It is now part of the elementary school.

Opposite, inset: An exterior look at the Morocco gym. Before it opened, the basketball games were played in the basement of the school.

"Back then the Chicago Bears would have their training camp in Rensselaer and [Bears' coach] George Halas would come over and talk to the boys," said Jim Lodes, who coached football and basketball from 1953 to 1957. "Everybody around here knew the Bears and liked football."

Morocco had a football field west of town with huge ninety-foot light poles. But all of that was taken away when the school consolidated with Mt. Ayr to form North Newton in 1967. The elementary school continued at the same site in Morocco and will for the foreseeable future. There are plans to add central air conditioning to the gym.

"I think our alumni are really happy it's going to stay," Storey said. "People here have such an identity with that school. Every year we have 275 to 300 people back for our alumni banquet. There's a lot of history there. We lose some of our alumni every year. But you don't want to lose that connection."

MT. OLYMPUS

On a quiet stretch of road on State Highway 65 on northeast Gibson County is the town of Mt. Olympus. It's hardly a town, and if there wasn't a sign denoting it, motorists would drive right past without a second thought.

"Just a wide spot in the road," said Mt. Olympus native Joe Coomer. "Not even that, really."

In busier times, back in the 1950s, there were two stores: a grocery store on the west edge of town and a gas station on the east. In between, on the north side of the highway, was the two-story brick school building. In the early days—Mt. Olympus became an Indiana High School Athletic Association member in 1919—the basketball teams played in the basement of the school in what later became the agriculture room.

Despite the school's small size, the Mountaineers enjoyed success. The 1929 team, led by coach Charles Robinson, won twenty-six consecutive games and the fourteen-team Owensville Sectional before losing to much larger Vincennes in the regional.

In 1939, a new gym was built to the east of the school as a Work Projects Administration project. Though its capacity was only a few hundred, the modern brick building rivaled anything in Gibson County. Through the two main entrance doors on the south were matching ticket booths and a narrow balcony with a railing that overlooked the floor.

"For a little country school, it was really something," said Coomer, a 1952 graduate. "Princeton's was bigger, but other than that ours was just as nice as any in Gibson County. It was a good school, too. That was back when everybody was involved in the community, and that really meant something to people."

The Mountaineers never again won a sectional, but they did have a moment of significance during the 1952–53 season when they defeated visiting and undefeated Evansville Lincoln, 39–38. Like all-black Crispus Attucks from Indianapolis, Evansville Lincoln typically was forced to play smaller country schools like Mt. Olympus.

"We were sitting there watching our [junior varsity] team warm up, and their varsity comes out on the other end," said Joe Thompson, class of 1953. "We're thinking, 'No way that can that be their second team.' We beat them, though. I still remember the farmers hollering from the balcony in their bib overalls."

Above: A new roof was put on the Mt. Olympus gym in 1990.

Opposite, inset: An exterior look at the Mt. Olympus gym in Gibson County, built as a Work Projects Administration project in 1939. It is now used for various activities, including wedding receptions.

The gym now appears to have been preserved from the time the high school was absorbed into Princeton in 1965. From the ticket booths, the scorer's table and the blue "M" at midcourt to the double ten-second lines and the "Mt. Olympus" etched in brick above the stage, not much has changed.

The school served kindergarten through fifth grade until 1970. It was razed, but the gym survived as a community center. A new roof was installed in 1990, and funds from the Lilly Endowment organization made it possible to make more improvements a few years later.

On one cool April evening, the gym was being prepared for a wedding reception.

"People weren't too happy when they closed the school," Thompson said. "But we did pretty well to keep the gym up like it is now."

MEDARYVILLE

Ralph Risner's motor sales company, going on forty years in business, is about the only remnant of what once was a bustling business district in the quaint Pulaski County community of Medaryville. Just south of Risner's store, sitting to the west of U.S. Route 421, was the brick schoolhouse, built in 1921 to replace the old school that became the Medaryville Garment Factory and operated from 1922 to 1996.

The Medaryville Black Horses were the pride of the community. Although the basketball team never won a sectional, an impressive new gym was erected directly west of the school in 1951. The new building had several classrooms under the gym, which featured large arching wooden beams and several rows of permanent bleachers on the east and west sides.

"Basketball was king in Medaryville," said Brian Capouch, who grew up on a farm near Medaryville and has researched the history of the community extensively. "People here were very proud of that gym and still are to this day."

Lonnie Steele played basketball at Medaryville and graduated from the school in 1958. His junior and senior seasons, Steele played for coach Art Windmiller, one of the colorful characters in Indiana high school basketball at the time.

"Back in those days there was a guy named 'Hooch' Manning who was sort of the 'downtown' coach," Steele said. "He had a lot of opinions [about] who should be playing and what plays we should be running. In the first half of one of our games at Medaryville my senior year, he was about three of our rows behind the bench and getting pretty loud. Windmiller had enough. He told our guard, Vernon Barnett, to throw the ball right at Manning's nose the next time down the floor. Sure enough, he did it. Popped him right in the nose."

It didn't take long for Manning to realize that the plan had come directly from Windmiller. He went after him and was escorted to the Medaryville jail.

"Windmiller felt bad about it and went down to the jail after the game," Steele said. "They became pretty good friends after that."

Medaryville consolidated with rival Francesville in 1968 to form West Central, which used the Medaryville gym for two more seasons until a new school was built. "WC" is still painted at midcourt in the gym.

The building is owned by the local American Legion, which has a bar in one of the former classrooms downstairs. The gym is still used on occasion for some community functions.

Steele came back and coached at Medaryville for several years, beginning in 1964.

"I really enjoyed little old Medaryville," he said. "I drove through it the other day with my wife, and we were talking about what a great community it was. So many businesses have left, like in a lot of small towns. But there are still some people there, like Ralph, who keeps it going in the proper direction."

The Medaryville Black Horses played in this gym until 1967. It was used for two more years after consolidation by West Central.

This gym in Medaryville is now owned by the American Legion.

An exterior look at the 1951 Medaryville gym in Pulaski County. There were classrooms located under the gym floor.

ROYAL CENTER

"If Milan can, we can."

That was the motto of the 1962–63 Royal Center Bulldogs, the final season before the school consolidated with Lucerne to form Pioneer. It was a smart, balanced and starless team that won the school's first and only regional.

"Not to brag, but I think the unique thing about that team was its intelligence," said Ed Schmaltz, a junior starter in '63. "I wasn't the only one that was on National Honor Society. But I always kid them that I was the only one to get a full-ride scholarship [to Tri-State University]."

Royal Center didn't make it as far as the 1954 Milan team, Indiana's most famous small school champion. After winning the Logansport Sectional (defeating the host Berries in the championship) and the Logansport Regional, Royal Center routed Greencastle 67–46 in the first game of the Lafayette Semistate. The run ended with an 81–66 loss to Lafayette Jeff in the semistate final.

"We didn't have any superstars, and our biggest player was maybe six four [junior Gerald Garrison]," said Berlin Rowe, who was in his fourth of five seasons at Royal Center in '63. "We didn't stall, but we played a controlled style of basketball. We were always working for a shot, but we were deliberate."

Royal Center played its home games in a gym built in 1939. The majority of the seating (approximately eight hundred capacity) was on the south side

the gym, with nine rows of permanent wood bleachers set behind a three-foot concrete wall. There were also five rows of permanent bleachers on the east and west ends. The team "benches" were on the stage, located on the north side. Temporary bleachers were also set behind the players on the stage, especially when the teams were playing well in the 1950s and '60s.

"The camaraderie in the town at that time was amazing," Schmaltz said. "It was a big deal. You knew everybody was pulling for you."

Unlike some of the ugly forced consolidations between rival schools at the time, the merger between Royal Center and Lucerne, located just four miles apart, was amiable.

"We all knew each other," said Ron Roller, who was a freshman the first year of the consolidation. "There weren't any hard feelings as far as I could tell."

The Pioneer teams played in the gym until the new school was built in 1967.

With most of its team back in 1963–64, the team made it to the regional championship, losing 64–62 to Valparaiso. That was the last season in Royal Center for Rowe, who went on to coach three years at Twin Lakes and seven years at Muncie Central.

Rowe and the '63 team were honored at a game in 1988.

"The five years at Royal Center was a great time," Rowe said. "Our family made lots of great friends there. It was a great place for basketball."

Above: Royal Center's gym in Cass County was built in 1939. Pioneer, a consolidation of Royal Center and Lucerne, played in this gym until 1967.

Opposite, inset: An exterior look at the Royal Center gym and school.

BURNETTSVILLE

When Jackson Township voted to build Burnettsville a gym in 1937, it was the final straw for neighboring Idaville. After years of bickering and feuding, the township split, and Idaville became part of Lincoln Township.

"The animosity isn't there anymore, but at one time it was pretty ugly," said Jeff Saylor, whose father, James Saylor, started a convenience supply company, J.H. Saylor, Inc., in 1947 in Burnettsville. "At one time, they were going to close the school in Burnettsville and move it to Idaville. That went over like a lead balloon. There were injunctions filed, and they did not end up closing the school. But when the new gymnasium was built, it was too much, and the township split."

With its relationship with Idaville precarious already, the people of Burnettsville went ahead with the gym. It was erected to the south of the 1903 two-story brick schoolhouse where there had once been an outside basketball court. The brick "Bee Hive" had six rows of bleachers on the north and south sides and a stage on the west end.

The school used the gym as its home court until 1963, when it consolidated with, ironically, Idaville and Monticello to form Twin Lakes. The property was used as a junior high until the early 1970s, when the school was torn down. For several years after that, the gym was home to a small manufacturing company, Myers Springs, until 1981. Walter Myers then donated the building and property to the town. The community received a grant a few years later to significantly upgrade the building, which includes a kitchen located under the stage.

"For the most part, it doesn't look a great deal different," said Saylors, who attended Burnettsville until the school consolidated after his freshman year. "The big curtain on the stage is gone, but not much else has changed."

The Burnettsville gym still has the double ten-second lines common in smaller gyms at that time. The original wood backboards also remain, as do the different sections denoted with paint on the brick interior walls.

The gym is still used for a variety of functions, including family reunions, alumni functions and other community events. In the early 1990s, Burnettsville and other area schools held a "Memory Lane" tournament similar to an old sectional. Burnettsville hosted a scrimmage game against Idaville.

"It was a lot of fun," said Larry McLeland, a 1956 Burnettsville graduate. "We even had the cheerleaders out for it. I hope we do that again, but we're all getting too old."

Above: The original wood backboards remain in the Burnettsville gym.

Opposite, inset: An exterior look at the Burnettsville gym in White County. It was built in 1937 and is now a community center.

STENDAL

Paul Hagemeyer was reading a book recently that chronicled the history of basketball in Indiana, specifically in the southern part of the state. Missing, though, was any reference to tiny Stendal in Pike County.

"Every school that made up Pike Central was mentioned but Stendal," said Hagemeyer, a 1954 Stendal graduate. "That really tore me up."

The Stendal Aces of the 1930s didn't have a gym of their own, practicing on two dirt courts outside the school, but they won three sectionals (1931, '32 and '39) in that decade. The team played its "home" games at nearby Winslow.

"There was a feed mill here in town which had a makeshift gym, and they would sometimes practice there in the upstairs part of it," Hagemeyer said. "But most of the time they were out on those dirt courts. It was fine in the cold, but when it got wet and muddy, that was a problem."

Stendal finally had a gym of its own built in 1949. Built for $36,000, it was located to the north of the three-story schoolhouse and dedicated on January 12, 1950. With five rows of wood bleachers on the north and south sides and a stage on the east end, it seated about three hundred people. It was small, but it was home.

"Back then, there were several businesses in town," said Leo Oxley, class of 1962. "There were few restaurants, a couple service stations, a funeral home.

But after the school was gone, it seemed like everybody picked up and left town."

Stendal, along with Spurgeon, consolidated into Winslow in 1966. All of the Pike County schools formed one school, Pike Central, in 1974.

But the community has retained some of its originality with its gym. In 1996, the community received a grant to renovate the building and tear down the old school, which had become an eyesore. Now a community center, the gym has much of its original charm, along with modern amenities.

"We've been able to turn it into something really nice for the community," said Hagemeyer, a retired educator. "It's useful for a lot of people."

Kern McGlothlin, a 1930 graduate, was one of Stendal's first standout players. He led the team to three straight Pike County championships as a player and later won 319 games in twenty-five seasons as a coach at Cynthiana, Stendal, Greencastle, Cannelton and Winslow. His 1949 team, led by Dick Farley, was undefeated until losing to eventual state champion Jasper in the sectional title game.

The original scoreboard at the Stendal gym was actually a hand-me-down from neighboring Holland.

"It was one of those wooden scoreboards that would flip over wooden panels for the score," Hagemeyer said. "It made a loud 'bang' when you'd pull the trip. I'd run that scoreboard when independent teams would play in that gym. Those were fun days."

Above: The Stendal gym in Pike County was renovated through a grant in 1996. It was built in 1949. Before that, Stendal played its home games at Winslow.

Opposite, inset: Stendal's teams practiced in a room above a feed mill before this gym was built in 1949.

LOOGOOTEE

Maybe no community in Indiana represents Hoosier Hysteria like Loogootee, a town of nearly three thousand people in southern Indiana. And maybe no person represents the spirit of basketball-crazy Loogootee like its longtime basketball coach, Jack Butcher.

Butcher is Indiana's all-time leader in coaching victories with 806, a mark that is recognized on the town's water tower. For forty-five seasons, from 1958 to 2002, Butcher roamed the Loogootee sidelines, leading one of the most successful programs in the state. The Lions had forty-two winning seasons and won twenty sectionals, eight regionals and two semistate titles in his tenure.

"We had some pretty good basketball teams," said Butcher, understating his role.

Butcher grew up in Loogootee and attended elementary school at St. John's, a Catholic school in town. St. John's didn't have a high school at the time, so he moved over to Loogootee's public school for his freshman year. At the time, in the late 1940s, the Loogootee Lions played their home games in their 1927 gym, proclaimed by the community as "the best small-town gymnasium in Indiana" when it was built.

The gym was a quintessential Indiana gym, with a wraparound balcony on three sides and a stage on one end. Even now, more than eighty years after it was built, the building still captures the essence of small school basketball.

"There's a certain kind of magic and nostalgia about those small, wooden bleacher gyms," Butcher said. "The kids would stomp their feet, and it would almost be deafening. I remember some of the fans would rather line up against the wall on that east end to harass the referees than sit in the bleachers. That crowd was so close to the floor."

Loogootee played in the gym until 1968, when a new gym was built. In later years, the gym fell into a bit of disrepair, which Butcher believed may have been by design.

"By that time we were playing some of our home games at different locations," he said. "We played Bloomfield at Shoals one time and played Bloomfield at the Hatchet House [in Washington] one year. Some of the bigger games got moved out. I remember once watching during practice as snow blew right through the cracks in the window. The ulterior motive was to convince fans that we needed a new gym. I think they let it run down a little bit for that reason."

Before 1927, Loogootee's teams played in a building that was built in 1903 by the Knights of Pythia and later became the Ritz Theatre. The new gym, which later became known as JFK Gymnasium, was dedicated on November 18, 1927. Admission was fifty cents, and the game was attended by Arthur Trester, commissioner of the Indiana High School Athletic Association.

The gym is now used for elementary and junior high practices.

"We've moved to a new gym and filled that one to the rafters," Butcher said. "We lost some of the noise and nostalgia. But it was time."

The Loogootee Lions played in this gym until 1968. It is now used for elementary and junior high practices.

Indiana High School Athletic Association commissioner Arthur Trester attended the dedication game at the Loogootee gym in 1927.

The Loogootee gym was hailed as "the best small-town gymnasium in Indiana" when it was built in 1927.

FORT BRANCH

When a lack of finances brought the future of the Fort Branch community center into question in the spring of 2010, Jack and Elvira Neidig, residents of Gibson County for more than sixty years, donated $10,000 to keep the facility operating.

"We didn't want to see them dispose of it, and the community needs it," Neidig said. "That money is enough to keep it afloat for a while, but we could use some more help. The heating bill runs quite high in the winter, so it'll help with expenses."

The gym was built in 1938 and was the home of the Fort Branch Twigs—noted above the ticket booth inside the west entrance—until the school consolidated with Haubstadt and Owensville into Gibson Southern in 1974. Unlike the gyms in those towns, which were purchased from the school corporation for one dollar by the respective communities after consolidation, Fort Branch is owned by a group from the town and operates on donations from alumni and fundraising ventures.

There were renovations made in 2000, but with no air conditioning and the high windows closed off by brick, the gym is toasty during the hot summer months.

"It's not designed to get very good ventilation and doesn't get used a lot during the summer," said Bill Ahlfeld, who has been on the community center board for more than twenty years. "Our basketball league numbers have been down some, and in the meantime, expenses and insurance have skyrocketed. We do a lot of little fundraisers to keep it going."

There are six rows of wood bleachers on both sides, with a section on the north side marked off for the pep squad. There is no seating on either end and little room between the end lines and a brick wall. When the gym was built, there were two large windows on the east end. The school, which was to the west of the gym, was torn down after consolidation.

Fort Branch was second-largest school in Gibson County behind Princeton, but it owned a decided advantage over the Tigers at one point in the late 1950s and early '60s.

"We won ten straight ballgames over Princeton, and only three of them were by more than two points," said Larry Holder, who coached the Twigs from 1956 to 1967. "The only school that wouldn't play us in our home gym (because of its size) was Princeton. When I got here, we played our home games against Princeton at Princeton. We got that changed and started playing them at Owensville."

Fort Branch won eight sectionals in all, four of them from 1959 to 1963. Many of those former players have contributed funds for the gym and have plaques hanging in the lobby inside the west doors.

"We're looking at other ways to raise the money we need to keep it up," Ahlfeld said. "It's a good gym. We just need to find a way to get as much use out of it as we can."

This gym was packed from 1949 to 1953 as the Fort Branch Twigs won four sectionals in that span.

An exterior look at the 1938 Fort Branch gym in Gibson County.

The Fort Branch Twigs called this gym home until 1974. The building stays open as a community center through donations and fundraising ventures.

KNIGHTSTOWN

S am Chase had been disconnected from his home state for more than twenty years, making only occasional visits, when in 1986 he was told about a movie that depicted high school basketball in Indiana in the 1950s.

Chase had starred at Knightstown in the late 1950s, helping the Panthers to a sectional title— the first in school history—as a sophomore in 1958. He left Knightstown with an armful of scoring records and went to a good career at LSU, where he played for former Muncie Central coach Jay McCreary. A six-foot guard, Chase turned down a chance to play in the fledgling American Basketball Association and went on to a successful career on Wall Street.

He was living in Georgia in 1986 when he decided to see what the fuss was all about with the movie. It took awhile for it to sink in that the gym portrayed as the home of the Hickory Huskers in the movie was the same one he'd played in nearly thirty years before.

"I was shocked," Chase said. "I immediately recognized it and became nostalgic pretty quick. There were certain scenes that brought me to tears. The one where dozens and dozens of cars follow the bus through the countryside was one. That was true. We'd have dozens and dozens of cars following our bus with their headlights on. The other was the scene in the locker room where they are all sitting under that one light bulb. We'd sat under that light bulb so many times before."

Thousands of fans visit the Knightstown gym—now known as the Historic Hoosier Gym—every year to see the fictional home of the Hickory Huskers, loosely based on the 1954 Milan team. Most remember Bobby Plump, whose last-second shot lifted Milan to the state championship over Muncie Central, and Jimmy Chitwood, the character played by Maris Valainis to portray Plump in the movie.

Though most of the visitors have never heard of Chase, many people in Knightstown have. He came back to Knightstown in 2006 for a parade honoring the twentieth anniversary of the movie. Chase was stunned by his reception.

"For whatever reason, life moving on I guess, I sort of divorced myself from my hometown and never really reconnected," he said. "I'd never realized that people would remember me or that our teams would have such a long-lasting impact. There were a lot of tearful moments."

The gym, built in 1922 and later renovated as a Works Progress Administration project in the 1930s, is used frequently for family reunions, pick-up games and birthday parties. But most people visit just to look around and get a sense of Indiana basketball in the 1950s.

"What you saw in the movie was pretty much how it was," said Larry Bundy, a 1960 graduate. "The only real difference was that the movie showed the team bench on the side and ours was on the end. But the crowd and the community involvement was all the same. It looked like it did back then."

An interior look at the Knightstown gym. The Hoosier Reunion Classic, played every June, features the top boys and girls seniors in the state.

Sam Chase was the all-time leading scorer in the Knightstown gym. He went on to play in college at Louisiana State University.

Opposite, inset: Looking east at the 1922 Knightstown gym. The home of the fictional Hickory Huskers in the movie *Hoosiers*, it is visited by thousands each year.

CAMDEN

After years of playing its sectional games in neighboring Carroll County communities—mostly Delphi and Flora—Camden thought it might get the chance to host when its new gym, which also contained several classrooms, a large shop area, a band room and a stage, was completed for the 1951–52 school year.

The new gym was impressive. Four Douglass fir arches, spanning 120 feet and weighing nine tons each, were shipped in from Maine. Built for $130,000, the gym could seat roughly fifteen hundred people for basketball games and more than twenty-two hundred for commencement and plays in a community of fewer than one thousand people.

But there would be no sectional games. The same year the gym was completed, the seven Carroll County schools were shipped to Kokomo for the tournament.

"We thought we were going to get the sectional," said Dick Kendall, a 1953 Camden graduate. "Then right when we built the gym, they moved it out. We finally had a gym with some room."

Before 1951, the Camden Red Devils played their games in a cracker box gym, added on to the east side of the school in 1920.

"It seated maybe two hundred people," said Max Rude, a 1955 Camden graduate. "The lines were right up against the wall. It got to the point you couldn't get other teams to come play you there."

Camden was noted for winning the longest game in state high school history when it defeated Delphi (at Delphi) 22–19 in seven overtimes in the 1935 sectional championship. The record stood for twenty-nine years.

The old brick school, built in 1899, was located to the west and south of the new gym. It was in the process of being demolished when it burned down on September 3, 1968. The gym and its surrounding classrooms—added on in 1966—were used for many years as an elementary school. Beginning in the 2009–10 school year, it was used for kindergarten only.

The last class graduated from Camden in 1965, when it consolidated into Delphi. Though the gym was only used for varsity basketball for fifteen seasons, it represents a time of big ambition when communities all over Indiana constructed gyms with capacities double and triple the towns' populations.

"If you're going to spend taxpayer money, you'd better have a good reason," Rude said. "There was a lot of excitement for it at the time."

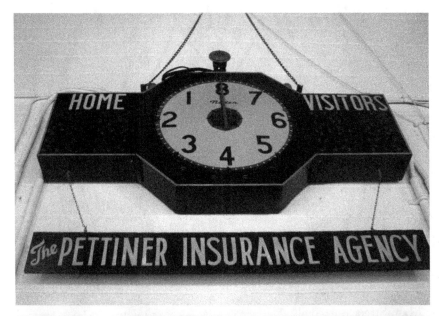

A scoreboard inside the Camden gym.

The Camden gym in Carroll County was opened in 1951. It is now used by kindergarten students, who go to school in the adjoining classrooms.

Opposite, inset: An exterior look at the Camden gym.
It was used for fifteen years by the Camden Red Devils.

STINESVILLE

Winfield "Dick" Jacobs was only five years old at the time, but he remembers the scene vividly. It was 1930, and the effects of the Depression had enveloped Stinesville, a small community tucked away in the hills of northwest Monroe County.

"Every man I knew was sitting on Main Street not doing anything," Jacobs said. "I asked my mom about it, and she said all those people had been laid off from the two stone mills in the area."

Stinesville was at the heart of the Indiana limestone industry, and many of the buildings along Main Street were built of limestone. The industry also spawned one of the great nicknames in Indiana high school sports: the "Quarry Lads" and "Quarry Lassies."

Stinesville's school burned down in 1935, and a new school was built the following year. It included a gym, which had a few rows of permanent wood bleachers on each side and high windows.

Jacobs, a 1943 Stinesville graduate, officiated basketball games for forty years, including the state finals in 1962, '63 and '64. He has endless stories about his days as a referee, but some of his best are from watching games at Stinesville as a kid.

"Stinesville didn't have a good reputation from the standpoint of its fans," he said. "Honest to god, I remember a game as a kid—this was probably 1937 or '38 at our home gym—when an older lady tripped a referee with her cane as he came by."

Jacobs recalled another story from that same time period when a referee was taken outside at halftime by a few locals and "busted up pretty good." The roughnecks then sent him back inside to officiate the second half.

"There were some tough nuts down there," Jacobs said. "Really, it probably wasn't any worse than other schools. In my own mind, I always knew the places where you'd have to be tough as hell [as a referee] when you walked on the court."

Stinesville combined with Ellettsville to form Edgewood in 1964. The former high school in Stinesville is now used as an elementary school, and the school's teams are still known as the Quarry Lads and Quarry Lassies. The gym has undergone extensive renovation since it was last a high school gym, including the addition of central air conditioning in 2009. The permanent bleachers were also taken out and replaced with retractable bleachers. A new room for a cafeteria was added on the north side of the gym in 1994.

Because of budget cuts and stretched finances, there has been talk of closing the Stinesville elementary school.

"People talk about budget cuts," said Kenny Barnes, a 1962 Stinesville graduate, "but I think children would be better off today if they were in smaller schools. There aren't as many cliques, and kids have good social lives. It wouldn't be good if we lost the school."

Above: The Stinesville gym was built in 1936. It is now used by the elementary school.

Opposite, inset: An exterior look at the Stinesville gym and school, now an elementary. The Stinesville Quarry Lads played their home games here until consolidation in 1964.

SPRINGVILLE

Jack Armstrong has a photo of himself, at age five, helping his father haul stone to the site of the new gym in Springville in 1936. Armstrong's father and several other area men loaded their trucks from Trinity Springs, located several miles to the south in Martin County, to Springville in Lawrence County.

The gym was built as a Works Progress Administration project, as many were at that time all over the state. Armstrong is quick to point out a unique feature of the gym, which is still evident today if you know to look for it.

"The first six feet or so of the gym, from the bottom, the stones are laid flat," he said. "After that, they decided they were making too slow of progress. Then you can see where they started laying the rocks on their edge."

Armstrong played in the gym as a youngster but never got the chance in high school. Springville was consolidated into Oolitic in 1942, and Armstrong graduated from Oolitic in 1949. Armstrong's older brother was part of one of Springville's last graduating classes with just five students.

"There weren't many boys to choose from to make up the basketball team," he said. "There wouldn't have been more than about fifteen boys in high school."

Springville was never a big town, although it once had a blacksmith, barbershop and hardware/grocery store that was a Walmart of its time. The gym was built on the north edge of town, directly west of the school. The school, a three-story brick building, was originally a house owned by a local doctor. It has since been demolished.

The gym has enjoyed a revitalization in recent years, with the help of a grant in 1998. The building is leased from the school corporation by Perry Township, which in turn leases it to Perry Township Volunteer Fire Department for $1 a year. With the help of about $70,000 of donated money, a group headed by fire department captain Dennis Godsey has cleared out a blighted area across the road from the gym and transformed it into a park.

"It's revitalized the community," said Armstrong, who now lives in Virginia. "That gym is right at the center of it."

The gym has been flooded several times by a creek that winds behind it to the west and south. The wood floor was finally taken out and a concrete floor poured. The center circle was saved and hangs in a meeting room on the gym's south side. There are six rows of wood bleachers on the north side, and there was originally a stage on the west end, but it has since been covered. Still, the gym retains much of its unique feel, especially late in the day when the sun shines through the high windows.

"I love to show it off," said Godsey, a 1964 Oolitic graduate. "We're pretty proud of it."

An exterior shot of the Springville gym in Lawrence County. It was built with stone from the area. Upgrades have been made with the help of a grant in 1998.

The Springville gym is available to rent. Springville only had a high school until 1942, when it was absorbed by Oolitic.

MOORES HILL

Living in the shadow of Milan—almost literally—wasn't easy in the 1950s. Moores Hill, located two miles east of Milan, the famous 1954 state championship team, didn't have the basketball pedigree of its neighbor.

Moores Hill watched from across the county line—Moores Hill is in Dearborn County, and Milan is in Ripley—as the Indians piled up eight sectional titles in the 1930s, '40s and '50s, including the state title in '54. Meanwhile, the Bobcats never won a sectional title. Moores Hill consolidated with Aurora and Dillsboro to form South Dearborn in 1978.

"We really got up for those games against Milan," said Butch Russell, class of 1959. "Probably too up. They wouldn't schedule us for a while; then we started playing them again later in the '50s. We had good enough teams, but they were always a little better."

Connecting the towns and basketball programs even further was the fact that Herman Grinstead, who was let go as coach at Milan in 1952 after ordering new uniforms without the superintendent's knowledge, came to Moores Hill in 1953 and coached there until his retirement in 1971.

Moores Hill had a unique history as a former college town. Moores Hill Male and Female Collegiate Institute opened in 1856 with about 150 students. The college grew too large for its original three-story brick building, and an appeal was made to businessman and entrepreneur Andrew Carnegie to provide financial support for a new school. He agreed to pay half of the $37,000 for the new building.

Built in 1907 and known as Carnegie Hall, the building still stands and is used for a variety of purposes, including a tearoom, a Head Start program, a museum and a gathering place for alumni functions. The college moved to Evansville in 1917—now known as the University of Evansville—but the building was used as a high school through 1978 and as elementary school until a new school opened next door in 1987.

The new school was attached to the gym, which was built directly west of Carnegie Hall in 1939. The floor originally ran north–south, with the main entrance on the north side of the building. During the renovation in 1987, a music room was attached to the north side, covering the main entrance. The bleachers, which had been permanent wood bleachers built in four sections, were replaced with retractable bleachers. The baskets were moved, and the floor now runs east–west.

Though Moores Hill never came close to matching Milan in basketball—it didn't win a single sectional game from 1966 to 1978—it wasn't so bad being in the shadow of a great story.

"Those were a great bunch of guys," Russell said of the '54 Milan team. "We could beat them in baseball. But basketball, they always had our number."

Carnegie Hall, located just east of the school and gym in Moores Hill, was built in 1907. It was a college until 1917, when it moved to Evansville to become what is now the University of Evansville.

The Moores Hill gym in Dearborn County was built in 1939. It is now an elementary school.

GREENSBURG

If you want to know what Greensburg's old gym looked like before it was renovated, look no farther than Rushville. The two gyms were built around the same time (the mid-1920s) with nearly an identical layout.

"I don't know who copied whose floor plan, but it's almost exactly the same," said Joe Westhafer, a 1954 Greensburg graduate.

The Greensburg gym was completed in time for the 1925–26 season and was used by the high school until a new school was built in the 1970s. Like Rushville, Greensburg's gym was a standalone brick building with entrances in all four corners. There was seating for more than three thousand fans all the way around the gym floor.

The seating arrangement, poor acoustics and overflow crowds (particularly at sectional time) created a unique atmosphere.

"Loud," said Bob Barker, a starter on Greensburg's regional champion teams of 1966 and '67. "I'll always remember how loud it was, especially when they played those sectional games there."

Greensburg hosted sectionals for many years, usually dominating the smaller Decatur County schools. From 1927 to 1967, the Pirates won twenty-four sectional championships. Several of the county schools played games at the Greensburg Armory, located just several hundred feet from the gym and also constructed in the 1920s.

"The county schools all hated Greensburg," said Westhafer, who later played at Florida State. "They all wanted to beat us more than anybody."

It was rare, though, that Greensburg got through the regional. The Pirates won the regional at Columbus in 1931 and '37 and, by the late '40s, were hosting the regional. The 1965–66 Greensburg team was probably its best, with four Division I players in the lineup. That team made it to the final game of the semistate (final eight teams) before losing 79–75 to Indianapolis Tech.

"We didn't start out great that year and lost seven games [20-7], but we really blossomed as the year went on," said Barker, who went on to play at Indiana State.

The old gym is now connected to a new junior high, which was renovated in 2008. It looks different, as there are walls at both ends instead of seats. The bleachers have been painted blue, but the old brown bleachers are still visible behind the wall on the west end.

"It was a heck of a nice building," Westhafer said. "Perfect for us."

Above: The Greensburg gym hosted many sectional tournaments in Decatur County through the years.

Opposite, inset: The Greensburg gym was built in 1925.

HUNTINGBURG

The people of Huntingburg know how to hang on to a gym.

The Huntingburg Memorial Gymnasium, dedicated in November 1951, seats more than six thousand fans—more than the population of the Dubois County community. Why so big? To steal the sectional away from rival Jasper, of course. It's logic only a Hoosier could truly appreciate.

Huntingburg hosted—and still hosts—various rounds of state tournament games at Memorial Gym. Filled to capacity, it represents the fervor of high school basketball in southern Indiana. When Nick Nolte was preparing to play a high school coach for the 1993 movie *Blue Chips*, then Indiana coach Bob Knight took him to a sectional at Huntingburg.

In the mid-2000s, a community group called the Friends of Memorial Gym raised more than $300,000 for extensive renovations to the gym, which should keep it sparkling long into this century for the Southridge Raiders, a 1972 consolidation of Huntingburg and Holland.

But the Memorial Gym isn't the oldest gym in Huntingburg; it's not even the oldest gym on its block. That honor belongs to the former home of the Huntingburg Happy Hunters, built in 1926. It originally had chair-back seats with a capacity of about eight hundred for basketball games. The school paper in 1924 said it would "be equal to any city of its size in Southern Indiana."

Today, only the outside resembles a gym. In 1998, a grant of $100,000 was secured by the Huntingburg Community Foundation from the Lilly Foundation to start renovations on the building, which had sat empty for nearly a decade.

A team of volunteers worked to upgrade the facility. It opened in October 1999 as the Teen Outback Center, which had originally been established in the mid-1940s but closed in 1991 because of the decaying building and a shortage of funds.

"There was talk that it was going to be torn down, but it was going to cost the school $80,000 or $90,000 to do it," said Ralph Begle, who helped spearhead the effort to save the gym. "We thought, 'What a waste that would be.' We raised $40,000 from the community, and with the grant, we were able to make some improvements."

Huntingburg wrested the sectional away from Jasper when the gym was built in 1926. It had bleachers on the north and south sides and a stage on the east end.

"It was an interesting gym," said Kenny Morgan, who graduated from

Above: The interior of what was the old Huntingburg gym. It was renovated in 1998 and is now used as the Teen Outback Center.

Opposite, inset: The 1926 Huntingburg gym in Dubois County is next door to Huntingburg Memorial Gymnasium, built in 1951, which seats more than six thousand fans.

Huntingburg in 1957. "It originally had foldout chairs, some of which we've been able to save, and they later put in bleachers in the 1940s. It had a lot of uses, such as the junior/senior prom, class plays, graduations. It was more than just basketball."

There is little evidence now that there was once a gym in the building. A large dance floor took the place of the gym floor, and a snack room replaced the locker room. There are also pool tables, arcade games and a large recreation room. Various youth groups rent the gym regularly; Begle said the building is in use roughly 165 days a year.

"They built the gym [the right way] in 1926," Begle said. "It's structurally sound; it just needed some work done to it. I think the community realized it still had a lot of potential."

ELLETTSVILLE

In basketball-crazy southern Indiana, Ellettsville had as good a thing going as any community from the mid-1930s to the early 1950s. From 1936 to 1952, a span of seventeen seasons, the Golden Eagles suffered just one losing season and won three of the school's four sectional championships.

"That was the golden era for us," said Marion Jacobs, class of 1950.

The Ellettsville teams of the early 1900s played on an outdoor dirt court when the weather was favorable and moved their games to a makeshift court at a seed mill when it wasn't. By 1920, games had been moved to a limestone building on South Street and, finally, to a made-for-basketball gymnasium as part of a school addition in 1926.

But that gym, which had just a few rows of bleachers on each side, proved too small. In 1936, Ellettsville dedicated a new gym that helped define the golden era of basketball in the Monroe County town.

"Very, very hot," Jacobs said of the Ellettsville gym. "We knew with that heat we could always wear down our opponents."

Warren Hanna, who graduated in 1942 and helped Ellettsville to a runner-up finish in the prestigious 128-team Wabash Valley Tournament that year, said he remembers elementary and junior kids sitting in the balcony that ran along the south side of the gym.

"We didn't lose very often there," said Hanna, who helped Ellettsville reach the semifinals of the twelve-team Bloomington Sectional as a senior.

The Golden Eagles finally won a sectional in 1947 and then broke through in a big way three years later. After winning the sectional at Bloomington, Ellettsville advanced to the regional at Martinsville. There, Ellettsville crushed Marco and Terre Haute Gerstmeyer by a combined fifty-four points. The first and only regional championship set off a wild scene back in Ellettsville.

"It was the craziest, wildest night that little community had seen since V-J Day," Bill Dyer of the *Bloomington Herald-Telephone* wrote. "Everybody was getting in everybody's way, and the whole crowd was deliriously happy. There were quite a few tears of happiness."

Left: The Ellettsville gym in Monroe County was built in 1936. The balcony has since been taken out.

Opposite, top inset: An exterior look at the Ellettsville gym. It is available to rent.

Opposite, bottom inset: A photo of the 1950 Ellettsville sectional championship team hangs in the gym.

The dream season was cut short in the Bloomington Semistate in a 56–43 loss to New Albany.

"That team had played together since the fourth grade," Jacobs said. "Our coach, Bob Wolfe, always wanted balanced scoring, and we had a team that played that way."

Ellettsville's 1936 gym still stands, although the balcony has been torn out, and pullout bleachers have replaced the permanent wood bleachers on both sides. The varsity team last used the gym in January 1965, when the new school and gym was constructed for Edgewood, a consolidation of Ellettsville and Stinesville.

Today, the gym and adjoining school are part of Eagle's Landing, which includes a number of local businesses. The gym is used for rentals, craft shows and, of all things, roller hockey practice. The building is owned by Kenton Robinson and his daughter, Beth Robinson-Pyclik. An oversized color picture of the 1950 team, its bright gold uniforms practically jumping out of the photo, hangs from the south wall inside the gym.

"You'd better believe people here still remember that team," said Richard Justis, a junior that season. "High school basketball was the number one thing back then. People don't forget."

DILLSBORO

Dillsboro's basketball past is buried beneath the pavement.

When a new elementary school was constructed in the Dearborn County community in 1989, the old Dillsboro high school building was demolished, and the belowground gym—built in 1922—was filled in with dirt.

"It was right about here," said Dillsboro elementary principal Bill Lakes, pointing to a spot on the pavement behind the school.

Dillsboro's basketball teams used the 1922 gym until a new wing, with a new gym, was added on in 1957. It was a necessary addition. Throughout the '50s, Dillsboro would practice in its basement gym with a concrete floor but had to move its home games to neighboring towns due to its size.

With its new, modern facility, Dillsboro was able to wrest the sectional away from Vevay in 1957. It was short-lived, though. Dillsboro hosted again in '58 and '59, but Rising Sun built a larger gym and took the sectional in 1960.

It was at the Rising Sun sectional in 1961 that the Dillsboro team had its most memorable moment. The Bulldogs, with a good, veteran team coached by Arlin Hooker, defeated North Dearborn by twenty-five points in the first round. But in the second game, Dillsboro was matched with Lawrenceburg, ranked number one much of the year and led by seven-foot center Jim Caldwell, who went on to play at Georgia Tech and in the ABA for the Kentucky Colonels. Lawrenceburg also had guard Ronnie Kennett, who went on to play at Kentucky.

Dillsboro upset Lawrenceburg 55–51 and then took out host Rising Sun 69–64 in the sectional championship.

"It wasn't our first encounter with that Lawrenceburg team," said John Race, a Dillsboro team manager in '61. "We were really familiar with them since we'd played one another and beat them in eighth grade. It wasn't luck that we beat them, but looking back it was kind of a shame they didn't get to go further."

Dillsboro, led by Bob Bockhorst, Jerry Edwards, John Snyder, Terry Kelch and John Luhrsen, hammered Connersville 90–65 at Connersville in the first game of the regional the following week.

"I was a junior at Brookville that year," Lakes said. "I remember being at Connersville for our sectional when they announced that Dillsboro had beat Connersville. I remember thinking, 'Where the heck is Dillsboro?'"

In the early 2000s, there was talk of tearing down the gym and building a new one as a smaller elementary gym. That potential move was quickly squashed. The permanent wood bleachers were taken out and replaced with retractable wood bleachers to make it more of a multipurpose gym.

"We ended up doing some structural strengthening to the building and basically built another gym all the way around it," Lakes said.

One thing that hasn't changed is the 1961 sectional team photo, celebrating its championship, hanging above one entrance of the gym.

"After the renovations, I told the workers we had to get it back up in the right spot," Lakes said, "or we'd get kicked out of town."

An exterior look at the Dillsboro gym.

The Dillsboro gym was built in 1957. Before it was built, the teams played in a basement gym, built in 1922, at the school.

MITCHELL

Indiana high school basketball was big in the 1950s. Bigger than college basketball in many places.

Max Ramey graduated from Mitchell in 1956 and went to the University of Tennessee on a basketball scholarship. He arrived in a world far different than the one he left behind.

"The gym at Tennessee seated about fifteen hundred fewer fans than our gym at Mitchell," Ramey said with a laugh. "Here I'd gone to a major university that had worse facilities than our high school. Basketball was not as big a deal at a lot of [Southeastern Conference] schools at that time."

Basketball was definitely a big deal in Mitchell, and the Blue Jackets had a gym to prove it. The school built a new gymnasium—with a capacity of more than three thousand—in 1927 to replace the much smaller gym inside the 1916 high school.

The gym had three levels of seating: several rows of wood bleachers on the floor, eight more rows of permanent seating with wooden benches and a balcony that ran along the north and south sides and the west end.

"There are things that you forget from that long ago," said Larry Ramey, who graduated the same year as his cousin Max in 1956. "But what you remember, and that's different than today, is that all of Mitchell stopped for basketball."

The new gym netted Mitchell the sectional in 1929, and the host site bounced back and forth between Mitchell

and Bedford for the next several years. For twenty-six straight years, from 1926 to 1951, either Mitchell (six) or Bedford (twenty) won the sectional.

The 1940 team was Mitchell's most successful. The Blue Jackets won the sectional at home that season, took the regional at Bedford and then won the Vincennes Semistate with a win over Lynnville and a 20–19 win over Washington. On March 30, 1940, Mitchell defeated Fort Wayne South Side in the afternoon at Butler Field House and then lost 33–21 to Hammond Tech for the state championship.

"I had two uncles on that team, Roy and Walter Ramey," Max Ramey said. "I wasn't old enough to see that team play, but they were an inspiration to me. I always heard stories about that team."

It would be another decade before Mitchell won another sectional, but the Blue Jackets' tradition continued into the 1950s under coach Bill Shepherd, who played under legendary coach Tony Hinkle at Butler. Shepherd coached nine years at Mitchell, winning sectionals in 1950 and '56.

"My sophomore year, we lost at home to number one Jeffersonville 53–51,"

At one time a balcony that ran along three sides of the Mitchell gym.

Left: This was the home of Mitchell's varsity teams until 1979.

Opposite, inset: The Mitchell gym was built in 1927 and replaced the smaller gym inside the school, which had been used since 1916.

Max Ramey said. "I remember it like it was yesterday."

Mitchell last used the gym for varsity basketball in 1979, although a high school game was played there in 1997–98 when the new gym was unavailable. The balcony has been taken out, and the stage on the east end was walled off. But on a June morning in 2010, eighth grade girls' teams from Mitchell and Orleans filled the gym—if not the bleachers—with sounds of basketball.

"That place is special to a lot of people," Larry Ramey said. "But what made it such a nice place was all the people that filled it up. Those people yelling at the referees from the front row—that's what made it fun."

CANNELTON

It's not basketball that first comes to Joe Hafele's mind when asked about the old Cannelton gym. It's a plane crash. More than fifty years later, it's an image he can't easily shake from his memory.

"The gym was a morgue," said Hafele, who was the basketball coach at Cannelton on March 17, 1960, when a Lockheed Electra turboprop, on a flight from Chicago to Miami, fell apart in midair and crashed several miles east of Cannelton, killing all sixty-three people on board.

Hafele, a 1946 Cannelton graduate, was in his tenth season as coach at the time of the crash. He assisted the state police in setting up its headquarters inside the gym. The wooden bleachers were covered with passengers' clothes recovered from the surrounding countryside when the plane nosedived a mile from the Ohio River, blowing a crater twenty-five feet deep into the earth.

"[The police] set up in the gym and came down through the fire escape with these rubber sacks filled with dirt," Hafele said. "They were looking for any semblance of human remains, but there really wasn't anything bigger than the palm of a hand. It wasn't as morbid as you'd think. The people had just disintegrated."

Life eventually got back to normal for Hafele. He coached at Cannelton until 1962 and stayed on as a teacher for twenty-two more years.

Not much changed in Cannelton. While consolidation swallowed up schools its size all over the state, Cannelton hung on. A

heated rivalry with Tell City, located just four miles north, made consolidation between the schools a near impossibility.

Cannelton kept its city-owned gym as well. Built in 1926, the brick building was quite large for its time, with seating for about eleven hundred fans. Through the front entrance on the south side, stairs led up to the floor. On either side were permanent wood bleachers, and there was a stage on the opposite (north) end. Below the gym, on ground level, there was at one time a fire department, the town hall and a library.

Cannelton hosted sectionals in 1928 and in alternate years with Tell City throughout the '30s and '40s. The Bulldogs won sectionals in 1933 (at home), '36, '46, '48 and '52.

"It was a nice place to play," Hafele said. "They had sock hops and school plays and bingo and dances there. It was sort of a community building."

The Bulldogs used it as their home court until 1998, when a new community building was constructed downtown. One of the five smallest schools in the state (there were eighteen students in the 2010

Above: Below the Cannelton gym was once a fire station. There are rooms now used as offices for administration.

Opposite, inset: An exterior look at the Cannelton gym, built in 1926. It was used as Cannelton's home gym until 1998. It is in need of repair, but there is no money in the budget.

graduating class), Cannelton has struggled in basketball for several years. Its last winning season came in 1991.

The gym is in need of renovation, but the cash-strapped school doesn't have the funds. Bleachers on the east side have been torn out, and the area is now used for an indoor batting cage.

"We'd never use it again for our high school team, but I'd like to get it to where we could use it for practices and maybe elementary or junior high games," said Cannelton superintendent Marion Chapman. "Estimates have been a half-million to a million dollars for what we need to get done. The gym is what I remember as old-time basketball. I just hate it that it's in the shape it's in. But it just always comes down to money when you're in a small district like we are."

ENGLISH

The town of English is gone. The Crawford County community exists on the state map, sure enough, and in reality. But it's not the original. In 1990, after another disastrous flood ravaged English, the community—with the help of state and federal funds—was moved more than a mile from its previous location.

It was a project that took eight years to complete but ensured that the three creeks and Little Blue River that surrounded English would no longer wreak havoc. Three holes of the Old English Golf Course now encompass what was once the downtown.

"The flood in 1979 was really bad," said Bob Roberts, eighty-two, a lifelong resident and 1945 graduate. "In three streets downtown there was probably eight to ten feet of water. A lot of people worked to build back up and then [in 1990] it got them again. That's when everybody decided enough was enough."

Two of the buildings demolished in the move were the first homesites of the English Red Raiders basketball teams. The original "gym" was a large room located above a drugstore. Two brothers, Felix Hammond, a dentist, and Guido Hammond, a doctor, owned the building and several others downtown. When it wasn't used as a gym, the building doubled as a skating rink for kids in English. It was later used as the Masonic Lodge.

The school used that building until 1930 and then didn't field another team until a

new community center was completed in 1939. When originally constructed, it was heated by two potbellied stoves on one side of the floor. It was a better situation than at Milltown, which had a stove located almost directly under one goal.

"You didn't dare drive on the south end," Roberts said.

The community center was built with donated labor from several community members.

"My dad was one of them who helped build it," said Steve Eastridge, a 1959 English graduate. "All the work and excavating was done by hand. We used to play in there every Saturday when I was growing up. One time one of the city fathers caught us in there playing in our street shoes, and I thought we were going to get killed."

The school was located east of downtown, out of the flood plain. The school, built in 1914, was a two-story brick building. A new school was built in 1955, with the addition of a new gym. It featured a rounded roof with several rows of permanent and pullout bleachers on both sides and a stage on the north end.

Above: All of the elementary schools in Crawford County use the old high school gyms, including this one in English. It was built in 1955.

Opposite, inset: An exterior look at the English gym.

"I played in our first game there, which was a junior varsity game before the varsity, against Birdseye," Eastridge said. "They packed it that night and for most games."

English and the other three Crawford County high schools—Leavenworth, Marengo and Milltown—consolidated to form Crawford County in 1976, but all the towns still have their own elementary schools. The English gym gained a tiny bit of notoriety in 1995 when it was shown briefly in the 1995 martial arts movie *Best of the Best 3: No Turning Back*.

The original town of English, like its first basketball gyms, is just a memory. A good memory.

"Going to those games as a kid…those guys were like gods to me," Eastridge said. "I worshipped them. I drive by the spot where that gym was every day and remember what that was like."

WEST COLLEGE CORNER

Shoot a half-court shot from Ohio and watch it swish through in Indiana.

The school and gym shared by the residents of College Corner, Ohio, and West College Corner, Indiana, make for one of the most unique, confusing and bizarre situations in the country.

College Corner and West College Corner are one community situated on the Ohio-Indiana state line five miles northwest of Oxford, Ohio. The school, built in 1925, is bisected by the state line of Ohio and Indiana. Midcourt of the gym is smack in the middle of the building, with an "I" painted on the west side of the center court circle and an "O" on the other.

"This is *the* state line," said Lynn Sheets, a 1966 College Corner grad and superintendent of Union County until he retired in the summer of 2010. "There's nothing like this. Back then you'd have a social studies course in Ohio and an English class in Indiana."

Outside the school, the inscription above one door is "Indiana" and the other is "Ohio." There were positives and negatives to such an arrangement, both in the community and at the school. The time difference was one that could go either way. Until 1961, the Indiana-Ohio border was the dividing line between the Eastern and Central Time Zones. And until 2006, Indiana did not observe daylight savings time.

"I dated a girl in high school from the Ohio side," said Sheets, who grew up a block from the school on the Indiana side. "I could get her home before midnight and I still had an hour because it was only eleven on my side—and I lived a block away."

Beyond the unique situation surrounding it, the gym has a classic look with double ten-second lines, an overhang balcony on one side and a stage on the other. As a kid, Sheets would watch games from the balcony, his feet dangling over the edge. Under the balcony were the team benches, the scorer's bench and several rows of bleacher seats for fans.

"We had a huge pep club," said 1970 graduate Maureen McDonough, principal of what is now the College Corner Union Elementary School. "Hard to believe in this tiny gym."

The school was featured in an episode of *Ripley's Believe It or Not!* in the 1980s. College Corner did not start playing games in the Indiana high school tournament until the 1928–29 season, and the Trojans never won a sectional. The team consolidated with Liberty into Union County in 1972. In 2009–10, there were 141 Ohio students in the school system.

"There are some unique gyms out there," said Sheets, standing at midcourt. "But the history of this one is something else. It's totally unique."

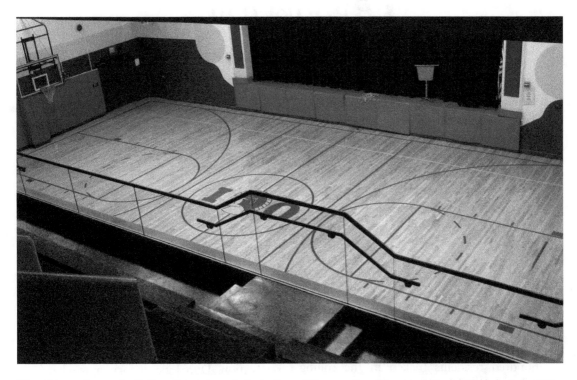

The midcourt line at the College Corner gym is the Indiana-Ohio state line. The gym and school were built in 1925.

An exterior look at the College Corner school.

Students from both Indiana and Ohio went to school here when it was a high school and still do now that it's an elementary school.

BROOKVILLE

After five years coaching at Vevay, John Collier was hired at Brookville in 1956 to resuscitate a program that had just won sectionals for the first time in thirty-three seasons and was playing in a small, outdated gymnasium.

Still, the demand to see Brookville's home games outweighed the seats available at the Lew Wallace Gym, built in 1931 at what was then the elementary school. Only partial season-ticket packages were offered.

"People in Brookville were clamoring for a new gym, and we did need it," Collier said.

In typical Indiana style, Brookville, a picturesque town of about twenty-seven hundred residents tucked in the rolling hills of Franklin County, constructed a three-thousand-capacity gym. In the first year it was open, 1957–58, Brookville went undefeated through the regular season and won the sectional at home.

"That was really something else," said Collier, who led Brookville to five sectional championships in ten years and a regional title in 1965. "We had some kids who worked pretty doggone hard and had a lot of success."

Brookville only hosted the sectional for one year; Connersville took it back in 1959, when its "Spartan Bowl" was completed. But the green-and-white Greyhounds gained a measure of revenge when they won the sectional again that year, including a 59–57, double-overtime

win over Connersville in the sectional semifinals.

The original Brookville gym was located in the basement of the two-story brick schoolhouse built in 1912. The county purchased the building from the school corporation in 2007. During the renovation, Don Jobe, a former teacher/coach/athletic director/superintendent at Brookville for forty years, discovered some relics of the old gym, which was converted to a cafeteria for many years.

"When they tore out the dropped ceiling, we found some of the original light fixtures for the gym and the two places where the baskets hooked on to the wall at each end," Jobe said. "People wondered how they played in there because the ceiling was so low. But originally, the floor was seven or eight feet farther down into the ground and later had been filled in. I have a couple friends in Brookville who played in that gym and say what a great gym it was."

The 1957 gym is located adjacent to the old school to the east; former classrooms under the gym are now

Above: Brookville hosted the sectional for one year after this gym was built. Connersville reclaimed the host site in 1959.

Opposite, inset: An exterior look at the Brookville gym in Franklin County. It opened in 1957.

occupied by Franklin County school corporation administrative offices. Brookville was consolidated into Franklin County—the only high school in the county—in 1989. The old high school gym is now used for junior high practices and games, and in a hallway outside the south entrance of the gym are large color photos of Brookville's sectional championship teams.

Collier left to coach Hanover College in 1966, where he stayed for the next twenty-five years.

"I have a lot of great memories of Brookville," Collier said. "The town was hungry for basketball. Even that year we built the new gym, we could barely handle the crowds. That undefeated team came back a couple years ago for a parade. It was quite an honor; it's hard to believe people remember you like that."

NEW CASTLE

One of Indiana's most famous high school games may have never happened—or at least would have happened in a different location—had fate not intervened.

It was around lunchtime on a June afternoon in 1959 when Ray Pavy took his father's car to check on the construction of the New Castle Field House, later labeled as the "largest and finest high school field house in the world" with a capacity of 9,325. Later that same day, the steel girders crashed into the massive hole that would later become the gym, halting the construction process.

Instead of opening for the 1959–60 season as anticipated, it was pushed back to the following season. Rather than playing his senior season in the new facility, it was back to the Church Street Gym—or "the Cracker Box" as many locals called it—for Pavy.

"I was a little disappointed, but when you're a kid, tomorrow is always a new day," Pavy said. "I was going back to a place I really loved to play. We knew we were going to be pretty good, and it was always fun to bring somebody in to play at the Church Street Gym."

The Church Street Gym was built in 1924 and was officially named after New Castle businessman Maurice Goodwin. The brick building located just east of the YMCA (and connected by an underground tunnel) was New Castle's

fourth gym. The first was used from 1909–11 and later became the Grand Theater; the second (1911–17) was on the second floor of the city building, above the city offices; and the third (1917–24) was the second floor of the old Sears building on Broad Street.

The Church Street Gym is cozy by today's standards. With a capacity of about eighteen hundred, fans were only able to buy season tickets for every other game. There were standing-room only tickets on the north end of the court, opposite the stage end, and also for aisle "seats." Pavy said the goal on the north end was about a half-inch lower than the south goal; New Castle always took the north goal in the second half.

The famous "Church Street Shootout" took place on February 20, 1959. It was

Left: The Church Street Gym in New Castle was built in 1924.

Opposite, top inset: This gym in New Castle could only seat about eighteen hundred fans. It was the site of the famous "Church Street Shootout" in 1959.

Opposite, bottom inset: The Church Street Gym in New Castle is now available for rent as part of the Henry Township Community Center.

the last regular season game played at the old gym and matched Kokomo, led by sharpshooter and Indiana Mr. Basketball Jimmy Rayl, against Pavy and New Castle. In a classic duel of future Indiana teammates, Pavy and Rayl combined for one hundred points. Rayl had fifty-one as New Castle earned a 92–81 win.

"I couldn't have imagined in my wildest dreams that people would still remember that game," Pavy said. "Rayl was maybe the best shooter of all time. Just unbelievable range. He would literally shoot it from half court."

Pavy joked that "about twenty-five thousand people" have told him they attended that game in 1959. He realized it was a big deal with legendary *Indianapolis Star* sportswriter Bob Collins called him the following morning.

The gym was a hub for many community events through the years and even had a tiny bowling alley in the basement at one time. The school had control of the building into the 1970s, when it was turned over to the YMCA. In the summer of 2010, it was under renovation, and it is available for rental as the Henry Township Community Center.

It seems odd now to think that the community with the largest high school gym in the country once played at a venue known as the Cracker Box.

"The spectators there were part of the game," Pavy said. "Our dressing rooms were right underneath the cheer block. And when that gym got rocking, you could literally feel it moving in that locker room. That's something I'll never forget."

UNION MILLS

When the Kelver family bought the Union Mills gym and adjoining classrooms in 1994 as a warehouse for their air heating and ventilations systems, the building was on the verge of collapse. The roof leaked, windows were busted out and knee-high weeds hugged the perimeter of the brick structure.

You'd never know it was once in such poor shape.

"It took some work," said Greg Kelver, president of Thermo-Cycler. "It was pretty far gone. But I think people here were glad we were able to get it fixed up."

The high school at Union Mills has long been gone, consolidated into South Central with Clinton Township and Hanna in 1962. The gym was constructed in 1951, attached to the 1898 schoolhouse (since demolished) on the north side. The old school had a tiny gym in the basement, with a ceiling that was barely higher than the top of the backboard. When the ball inevitably hit the ceiling, plaster would fall onto the floor, and the game would have to be stopped.

"It was unsafe," said Glen Rosenbaum, a 1954 graduate. "The hard cement walls were close to the court, and there weren't many seats at all. After my brother Ray's senior year in 1950, they condemned the gym, and we played our home games at some of the other small gyms in the area."

There was an outcry for a new gym even in the 1930s and '40s. Carl Sanders, a teacher and coach at Union Mills from 1934 to 1942 penned a column called "Off County Backboards" for the *LaPorte Herald-Argus*. His last column before leaving to serve in World War II called for Union Mills and other schools in the county to build new, safer gyms.

The final Millers' team to play in the old gym was also its most memorable. Tiny Union Mills won the enormous sixteen-team sectional—its first and only in school history—with a 54–44 win over host Michigan City in the championship.

"My brother was about six two and 180 or 190 pounds and had a left-handed hook shot he could hit from the free throw line," Glen Rosenbaum said.

Union Mills was known more for its baseball teams than basketball, and Glen Rosenbaum was probably its top product. He was picked up by the Chicago White Sox out of high school and cut the last day of spring training when he was nineteen. He pitched in three big league camps but spent all eleven years of his career in the minor leagues. Rosenbaum was 100-42 for his career and spent another twenty-nine years with the big league team as the batting practice pitcher and, later, the traveling secretary. He lived in Union Mills the entire time.

The gym where Rosenbaum once played basketball looks game ready. Boxes of heating systems cover the wood floor, but the original baskets remain attached on both ends.

"There's a lot of memories in that gym," he said. "It was so tough to see the town lose the school, like a lot of places. I still remember standing on a chair in the kitchen of our farm listening to the Milan [championship] game in 1954. We had an old Zenith radio on top of our refrigerator. I stood there and listened to every second. It meant too much to the small-town schools for that to happen."

An outside look at the Union Mills gym in LaPorte County. It was built in 1951.

The former Union Mills gym is now used as a warehouse for air heating and ventilation systems.

MT. ST. FRANCIS

Outside of the folks in Floyd County—and probably not all that many of them—few people had even heard of tiny Mt. St. Francis Seminary before 1948. The school of sixty-three students produced one of the more stunning stories in the Indiana high school basketball tournament that year, in its first year in the state tourney, by winning the fifteen-team Paoli Sectional.

Before the 1943 season, the Indiana High School Athletic Association did not allow Catholic schools to participate in the tournament. But the Mt. St. Francis coach, Father Hilary Gottbrath, did not enter his team until 1947–48, when he felt it was ready. The Vikings had a nice regular season, finishing 9-5. But two of the losses were to possible sectional opponent Morgan Township by a combined forty-eight points.

"We always had pretty good teams," said Father Howard Hansen, a junior on the 1948 team. "But we just didn't have very many students to choose from."

Located five miles northwest of New Albany, Mt. St. Francis was made up of students from different parts of the country studying for the priesthood. On October 11, 1923, the dedication of a three-story brick building marked the growth of the seminary. There were dormitories for about one hundred students on the third floor, a study area with classrooms and meeting rooms on the second floor and a kitchen, a boiler room and a (very small) gymnasium on the lower floor.

Though it was considered one of the nicest facilities in the area in 1923, the basement gym had a floor that was just fifty-eight feet long and thirty-nine feet wide. But the most distinctive features were the low ceiling (barely three feet above the top of the backboard) and the lack of spectator seating. There

was—and still is—a platform for seating through the doors on the south end of the gym. A row of seats was also set up along the east wall, and the teams sat on a bench under the platform on the south end.

It was cozy inside the Mt. St. Francis gym on game nights.

"You couldn't get very many people in there at all," said Brother Larry Eberhardt, a 1954 graduate and now the archivist at Mt. St. Francis. "There were three rows of bleachers on that platform and a row along the side, and that's all that could come to see a game. It worked for a while."

The '48 team defeated New Salisbury 55–53 in the first round of the sectional, defeated English by twenty-four points in the second round and upset Morgan Township 48–43 in the semifinals. The "Fighting Franciscans" then knocked off favored French Lick 43–42 in the championship game.

A story in the *New Albany Valley News* after the sectional championship noted the unusual shooting technique of the Mt. St. Francis players. "They seldom arch shots—just shoot straight for the basket," wrote Wally Criswell. "Every shot that goes through the hoop seems to actually tear the nets. The reason for this method of firing came about because of the low ceiling in the Mt. St. Francis gymnasium. It's impossible to high arch a ball and the boys naturally have to aim straight away and shoot by the same method."

Father Hansen said recently, "Everyone else hit the ceiling when they shot. We didn't because we knew how to shoot in there. It was an advantage for us."

The Vikings again won the sectional in 1951, defeating Marengo in the championship. The school closed in 1975, although the gym is still used by youth teams in the area.

An exterior look at the Mt. St. Francis gym in Floyd County.

The Mt. St. Francis team started playing in the state tournament in 1948 and won a sectional.

There was very little seating inside the Mt. St. Francis gym. It was built in 1923.

CHILI

Since its final days as a high school in 1961, the Chili gym in Miami County has undergone several reincarnations: as an elementary school (until 1973), a community center, a church and a flea market. For the last fourteen years, Tom Davis and his wife, Vicki, have turned the old gym into their home.

It has taken a little time for people to get used to that idea.

"For a while people would just walk up and come into the house," said Davis, the sports editor at the *Fort Wayne News-Sentinel*. "They thought it was still a flea market. I'd be sitting here in the couch on a Saturday afternoon watching Notre Dame football and somebody walks right in. That was kind of bizarre. But that stopped after a couple years; word spreads in a small community."

When originally built in 1925, the gym resembled a white barn. There was a coal stove just a few feet from the wood playing floor in the northeast corner, a few rows of permanent wood bleachers on the west side of the court and a stage on the north end.

Davis, who had no construction background, bought the gym on something of a whim. He and his wife were living in the Indianapolis area and wanted to get closer to Vicki's family, who live in Miami County.

Projects to "fix up" the old gym are constantly ongoing, most recently entailing the addition of a new roof. Bedrooms have been added on the east side of the floor, and the stage is now a living room area. The two-story brick schoolhouse, which was directly west of the gym, was demolished several years ago.

"People are really happy somebody is doing something with it," he said. "There was talk that it might be torn down."

The Chili Polar Bears never won a sectional but had strong teams in the 1950s under Bob Macy, an Indiana Basketball Hall of Fame member as a player (Converse, 1944) and coach. He got his first coaching job at Chili in 1950 and stayed five years. He later coached at Peru, and his son, Kyle, was Indiana's Mr. Basketball in 1975.

Chili won the Miami County Tournament in 1954 and lost just one game in the regular season. But for most of Macy's tenure—and until the school was consolidated into North Miami in 1961—the Polar Bears rarely used the gym for their home games (only twice in 1952–53 and 1953–54), instead going seven miles north to Gilead, which had a larger gym.

"We didn't mind playing in our gym, but Bob Macy felt like we should play on bigger courts to help prepare us for sectionals," said Galen Smith, a 1954 graduate. "It was a unique gym, some in good ways and some not so good."

Crispus Attucks, an all-black Indianapolis school at the time, played a game at Chili in 1940. Attucks struggled to find games and often traveled several hours to small Indiana towns. In 1943, World War II draftees were processed in the gym.

Occasionally, Davis will still get an interested old-timer showing up on his porch hoping to take a look around.

"I think they're happy just to know it's still here," he said.

Above: An exterior look at the 1925 Chili gym in Miami County.

Below, left: The former Chili gym is now the home of Tom Davis and his family.

Below, right: Chili moved its home games north to Gilead in the 1950s.

MICHIGAN CITY ELSTON

The Red Devils basketball team owned Michigan City in 1965–66. They had for a while, really. But that season was different. Instead of winning the sectional—like "City" had done for the previous fourteen years—and losing in the regional, mostly to Hammond, Gary Roosevelt or East Chicago Washington, this team finally broke through.

Michigan City celebrated. And celebrated. And celebrated again.

"When we beat South Bend Central in the regional championship at Elkhart, everybody packed into the Elston gym around midnight for a pep session," said Warren Jones, the principal from 1963 to 1977. "Then we went to Fort Wayne the next week for the semistate, beat Kokomo and Anderson and came back to the Elston gym for another pep session well after midnight. When we beat East Chicago Washington and Tech in the state finals [at Hinkle Field House], there wasn't enough room in the gym for a pep session. We had ten to twelve thousand people out at Ames Field to celebrate."

The '66 team was a culmination of many successful but frustrating years. From the early '60s on, there was rarely an empty seat in the Elston gym, built in 1937. In fact, modifications were made to the gym, including adding bleacher seating on the stage, to increase capacity from twenty-five hundred to roughly forty-two hundred. Even then it wasn't enough.

"Everybody wanted to be a Red Devil," said Larry "Hoppy" Gipson, a starting junior guard in '66. "That was *the* ticket in town. The crowds were rowdy and into it. You look back at that time and appreciate what a great time that was."

Doug Adams, who began coaching at Elston in 1957, was known for his explosive yet balanced teams. The 1965–66 edition, with a strong bench and six-foot-six Terry Morse in the middle, was no different. The team started slow, with a 6-3 record, but won its final twenty games. Jim Cadwell was the Trester Mental Attitude Award winner and scored a team-high twenty-one points in the 63–52 title game win over Tech, but Morse, Gipson, Rob McFarland and O'Neil Simmons all played key roles throughout the season.

"His philosophy was to have teams that were really well balanced," said Al Whitlow, a longtime assistant of Adams. "One thing he struggled with was when we got close to one hundred points; he didn't want to get to one hundred and embarrass the other team. We'd have our third line

Above: The Michigan City Elston gym was built in 1937. It was used by the high school team until 1995, when Elston and Michigan City Rogers merged. It is now used by the junior high.

Opposite, inset: An exterior look at the Michigan City Elston gym in LaPorte County.

guys in there shooting with the wrong hand. But he finally got over that. We had a coaches' meeting one day, and he said that we'd just turn them loose."

The Michigan City high school split in 1971 when Michigan City Rogers formed. Elston continued until 1995, when the school was merged back together and became known as the Michigan City Wolves. The old Elston gym, now used by the middle school, looks virtually the same as it did in 1966, except for the floor, which is outlined in blue paint instead of red.

"It's probably been fifteen years since I've been in there," said Gipson, who played at Indiana and still lives in Michigan City. "I'll get back sooner or later. That was a special time. After we won the state championship, the celebration lasted for weeks. It was like it was never going to end."

SIDNEY

Bill Patrick's coaching career—still going into its forty-second year as of the 2010–11 season—spans generations. He started at his alma mater, Sidney, in 1963.

The game was different in many ways, including the venues where his teams played. The gym at Sidney, built in 1922, was a true cracker box. The first Sidney teams in the early 1900s played on the second floor of a hardware store.

By the time Patrick came back to coach at the school (he graduated from Sidney in 1956), his teams were playing their home games a few miles up the road at Pierceton.

"More and more schools at that time had newer gyms and didn't want to play in the smaller ones anymore," Patrick said. "Most of the time we practiced at Pierceton, too. We'd get over there at 6:00 a.m. before school and practice. Most of our kids were from the farm, so they didn't mind getting up early so they could work on the farm after school."

The Sidney Wildcats played most of their games in the home gym until 1962. There were just a few rows of bleachers on each side and a stage on the north end. The wall on the south end butted up against the out-of-bounds line, and an eighteen-foot-high ceiling didn't leave much room for a high-arcing shot. It was better than the situation at nearby Burket, though, where shots were routinely rejected by the low rafters.

"People would stand in the doorways at Sidney because there was no room to sit," said Barb Slater, a former cheerleader and 1951 graduate who operates a market in

Sidney with her husband, Harold. "The stage was always full of kids."

One drawback was the locker rooms. Both teams had to leave the gym and go down the same stairway to get there. Bad blood sometimes boiled over on the way there.

"We played some independent league games there when I was coaching, and after the game there was typically some pushing and shoving," Patrick said. "There wasn't much that separated the teams. Then when you got down there, the showers were usually cold."

Patrick, who was inducted into the Indiana Basketball Hall of Fame in 2008, estimated the gym's capacity at about three hundred. But his graduating class was just thirteen, and most classes were fewer than twenty.

"Basketball was fun," he said. "I'm not sure kids now have that much fun. I wish all the coaches now would have had the opportunity to coach back then. The whole community supported the program because it was theirs."

The gym is now owned by Lee Weyant, who lives in the 1958 addition to the east of the high school that was originally built as an elementary school. Weyant rents the

The Sidney Wildcats played most of their home games here until 1962.

Right: The Sidney gym in Kosciusko County was built in 1922. It is now used as a flea market.

Opposite, inset: An exterior look at the Sidney gym.

gym out as a flea market. The basketball goals still hang from both ends of the court.

"When Indiana high school basketball was at its best, gyms like Sidney's were fun to play in," Patrick said. "It wasn't big, but when you were out there playing, you never thought about the size of the gym. You just had to have some outside shooters because a zone defense could pretty well cover one side of the court."

PIERCETON

Pierceton was mostly known in athletics for its standout baseball teams. But the school in Kosciusko County in northern Indiana also produced some memories in basketball, before the school was consolidated into Whitko with Larwill and South Whitley in 1971.

The Cubs' home gym was built in 1927, similar in style to that of Fort Wayne North Side, with three five-foot walls around the perimeter of the court and a stage on the south side.

"It was kind of like playing down in a pit," said Jack Horn, an all-county guard in 1956–57. "You went down a ramp to get into the gym, and then all the seats were up above you."

The gym's look now—it's part of an elementary school in the Whitko Corporation—bears little resemblance to its look when first constructed. The dangerous walls have been taken out, and there are retractable bleachers on one side. The stage remains one of the few original features.

"When you walked in the front doors [on the east side] you [would] walk in between the bleachers and then go up the steps to your seat," said Phil Menzie, a 1969 graduate. "It's completely different now. You can't really tell what it used to look like."

Pierceton won sectionals in 1928, '41 and Horn's senior year, '57. The sectional had moved from the armory in Warsaw to the new gym at Syracuse in 1956, and Warsaw defeated the Cubs 61–55 in the semifinals. Pierceton cruised into the sectional championship with three double-digit wins and then defeated Etna Green 63–60 to take the title.

Pierceton won again the following week in the regional semifinal at Plymouth, defeating Plymouth 51–49. The ride ended there. South Bend Central, the eventual state champions, led by Indiana Mr. Basketball John Coalman, defeated the Cubs 89–42.

"We led after the first quarter," Horn remembered. "They just overpowered us. We were a small team and didn't like to stall. That was probably our hope. But we figured, 'We're going to lose our way.'"

Horn was part of the first Kosciusko County Hall of Fame induction class in 2009. Though the walls are down, the Pierceton gym is still a special place for Horn.

"Let me put it this way, if you were going to foul somebody back then, you hammered them," he said. "And that wall was only eight or ten feet away from the court. It was kind of a dangerous place."

Above: The Pierceton gym has been renovated since it was built in 1927. It is now used by the elementary school. At one time, there was a five-foot wall around three sides.

Opposite, inset: An exterior look at the Pierceton gym in Kosciusko County.

FREETOWN

It was easy to know when there was a big game going on at Freetown: just count the faces in the windows.

The Freetown gym, at maximum, held about four hundred people. Until 1931, the basketball teams practiced on a dirt court in Freetown or, when available, in the Brownstown gym. Sherman Berry, a local businessman, donated the lumber from his flowering mill on the north side of Freetown for a new gym downtown. Berry owned the gym, which resembled a white barn from the outside, until the late 1940s.

"I was sitting in study hall one day, and a woman from Berry's company came in and told our principal, Fred Brock, that we weren't going to be able to play our game that night because we hadn't paid the rent," said Dean Zike, class of 1948. "He must have paid because we went ahead and played."

Freetown's only sectional championship was in 1925, but the Spartans fielded several strong teams in the 1930s, '40s and '50s. Edgar Sprague coached from 1932 to 1948, missing three years in that span due to his service in World War II. But he was instrumental in bringing Crispus Attucks, an all-black school in Indianapolis, to play games at Freetown in the late '40s (Freetown also played at Attucks).

"If you could ask everybody on our team right now, Crispus Attucks was the best sports we ever played against," said Jim Fields, class of 1949. "If they knocked you down, they'd help you up off the floor. They'd put their hip into you, and we'd do it to them, but they were fun to play against."

The game against Attucks drew a crowd—too big a crowd. Like the game against Vallonia the year before, some fans watched the game out in the cold from the roof windows.

"There were quite a few of them up there, too," said Zike, who came back and coached at Freetown from 1955 to 1960. "Not everybody could get in for those big games."

Bill Brown, a left-handed post player, was Freetown's top player in the late '40s. In 1948, the Spartans went 18-7 but lost in the sectional championship to host Seymour by twenty points. Freetown knocked out Seymour the following year in the semifinals but lost 48–38 to Medora in the championship. The team struggled again for several years until a team coached by Zike in 1958 went 20-4 and again lost to Seymour in the sectional championship.

Though the team had started to play its home games elsewhere by the late 1950s, Freetown kept its gym. It underwent a $550,000 renovation with the aid of a grant in 2003. The upgrade was significant for a building that was beginning to collapse on the east side. It is used now as a community center and is available for rent. The gym looks generally the same on the inside, although the stories from its heyday probably wouldn't fly today.

"One night we're playing Medora in our gym, and they have a coach named Earl Chambers who had been around a long time, coaching at Paoli and Brownstown," Zike said. "Before the game, he got out a stepladder and started measuring our rims. We just watched him. He said one was an inch too low, and he said our rims weren't level. He knew I had the better team. So we're beating them in the second half, and during a timeout I see him standing in our huddle. I asked him what he was doing, and he said, 'These boys don't understand me, I thought I'd come over and see what you had to say.'"

An exterior look at the Freetown gym, built in 1931.

The Freetown gym in Jackson County has been refurbished.

HONEYVILLE

None of Leroy Lambright's ten brothers and sisters went to school beyond age sixteen, as was the custom for Amish-raised children at the time. Lambright likely would have dropped out as well if it weren't for basketball.

"I was the tenth of eleven kids, and the older kids quit at sixteen to help out on the farm," said Lambright, a 1958 graduate of Topeka, located in Northern Indiana's LaGrange County. "In elementary school, I was quite involved in basketball and continued to be that way. My folks never said anything about [dropping out of school], so I just kept going."

Lambright continued on as one of the top players for the Topeka Bears in the 1950s. He scored 1,257 points in his career, a mark that stood as a county record until Westview's Gary Yoder broke it in 1973.

Lambright grew up in an area that was—and still is—largely Amish. He attended elementary school in Honeyville, an unincorporated town that was little more than a cluster of homes with a popular hangout that was part drugstore, part convenience store and part restaurant. In 1930, about a half mile east of the town, a new school was built for the Eden Township students that at one time housed up through the ninth grade. Shortly after it was built, Topeka—located about six miles to the southeast—began using the tiny gym as its home court.

"Topeka had a gym," Lambright said. "But it was barely more than an oversized hallway with classrooms around it. They used it for the high school gym in the 1920s, but it was way too small."

Topeka played its games and practiced at the Honeyville gym. It stayed that way until 1963, when the school began its consolidation with Shipshewanna.

The gym in Honeyville had permanent seating on the south side, with folding chairs set up on the stage on the north side. Capacity, at most, was about four hundred people.

"I played there my freshman and sophomore years," said Keith Bobeck, a 1958 graduate. "We had really small classes, but the gym was generally full all the time."

Because of the high Amish population, Topeka sometimes struggled with numbers compared to competing schools.

"We had some really good teams when I was in elementary school, but the Amish kids didn't stay in school back then," Lambright said. "That's just how it was. There just weren't a lot of kids to pick from."

The gym is now used by a church, the Eden Worship Center. The church tore out the bleachers recently and plans to take down the baskets soon.

"It was a charming little place," Lambright said. "You knew everybody there. Our teams were never really that good, but it was still a social event on basketball nights. It was a community event."

An outside look at the Honeyville gym.

Topeka played its games in the Honeyville gym, built in 1930. It is now used by a church, the Eden Worship Center.

VERSAILLES

The address for Tyson Auditorium was Versailles, but in the 1950s the building really belonged to all the small schools in Ripley County. Included in that group were the 1952–53 and 1953–54 Milan teams.

"My senior year we only played one home game at Milan," said Bobby Plump, who hit the famous shot to beat Muncie Central 32–30 in the '54 state championship. "The rest of our home games were at Versailles. And my junior year we played all but three of our home games there. It was like our home gym. [Former Versailles coach William "Gus" Moorhead] told me many times he was damn sorry he loaned us that gym. I told him we appreciated the home court advantage."

Tyson Auditorium was the site of many big games in Ripley County through its last hurrah in 2008. It was constructed in 1950 at a cost of $178,000 and had a seating capacity of twenty-two hundred. More than half of the cost was covered through the trust fund of James Tyson, one of the founders of Walgreen Drug Company. The distinguishing feature of Tyson Auditorium was its limestone exterior and cream-colored brick.

Moorhead, who came to Versailles in 1951 right out of Hanover College, called Tyson Auditorium "a palace" and considered it one of the main attractions in coming to Versailles. Moorhead coached at Versailles until 1966, when it consolidated into South Ripley, and then stayed on for two years at that school. He died in 2008.

"We had a little three-month-old girl at the time we came up there to interview," said his widow, Mary Margaret Moorhead. "It was such a thrill to see that gym and think he could possibly get his first coaching job there."

Despite a new gym and a new coach, Versailles was not exactly a basketball power. The Lions had last won a sectional in 1928 and had reputation for "uptown coaches" who could be difficult to please.

"Gus was one of those people who wasn't troubled by what other people said and didn't hang out in the places where they could get to him," Mary Margaret Moorhead said.

Instead, Moorhead spent most of his waking hours at Tyson Auditorium. On many winter nights, his wife would bring him dinner at the gym. Although Versailles lost seven games to Milan in two seasons—Plump's junior and senior years—success was right around the corner. In 1957, playing at home, Versailles won the sectional for the first time in twenty-nine years.

Above: The Tyson Auditorium in Versailles was built in 1950. The state championship Milan team of 1954 used it as its home gym.

Opposite, inset: An exterior look at the Tyson Auditorium in Versailles. It was used by the South Ripley high school teams until 2008.

"It was so loud during that sectional tournament that we had to go down in a little runway that led to the locker room during timeouts to hear [Moorhead]," said Don Lostutter, a 1957 grad. "After we won, a snake line went through town, though all the taverns and the streets."

It was the first of four consecutive sectionals won by Versailles. The sectional moved to Milan in 1960, when a new gym was built there.

Today, the adjoining school has been renovated into apartments. There are plans to turn Tyson Auditorium into a community center.

"To me, at that time, it was one of the marvels of the world," Plump said. "We didn't play on any regulation floors like at Tyson. I have great memories of that place."

MADISON

In 1939, Ray Eddy arrived from another Ohio River town, Tell City, just five years removed from his playing days at Purdue, where he played alongside coaching legend John Wooden. When Eddy left eleven years later to return to Purdue as coach, he had forever changed how basketball was viewed in Madison.

"Nobody called him his first name—it was Mr. Eddy," said Andy Taff, a 1943 Madison graduate. "He was strict. Not only with basketball, but with schoolwork. You had to give him a report card every six weeks, and if the grades weren't what they should be, you didn't play. He changed basketball in Madison. There were some good players that came along, but he was the No. 1 reason why it changed."

The Madison Cubs had been a program on the rise in the 1930s, in part because of a new basketball facility. The Brown Memorial Gymnasium, situated just one block from the Ohio River, made its debut on February 27, 1925. It was built at a cost of $50,000 and financed completely by J. Graham Brown, a Madison native who made his money in the lumber business. With seating for about thirteen hundred people, it was the biggest in the area. Less than a month after it was dedicated, Madison hosted the 1925 sectional.

Madison's basketball pedigree didn't take hold until 1933, when the program won its first sectional. The Cubs won four more in the next five years. But when the Ohio River flooded in 1937, the water rose to four feet inside Brown Gym and ruined the wood floor (to this day, a mark on the brick outside the gym notes the water level of the '37 flood). The sectional was moved to Scottsburg for a year until the gym could be renovated. The "new" gym featured a floor that ran north and south instead of east and west and permanent wood bleachers around three sides.

"They were able to add about one thousand seats, and it was one of the first gyms that didn't have the steel supports that obstructed people's view," said Spence Schnaitter, a 1950 graduate.

Eddy came to Madison the following year and started a run that saw his teams win six regionals in eleven years, a remarkable achievement with more than seven hundred schools playing in one tournament at the time. Madison was state runner-up in 1941 and '49 before winning it all in 1950.

"He came here and won immediately, and the fans became rabid pretty quickly," said Ed Orrill, a senior on the '49 team. "He just kept adding on to it. It was really remarkable."

Above the front door today, the inscription reads "Brown Memorial Gymnasium, Home of the 1950 State Champs, Ray Eddy Coach." The gym was used by the Cubs until a new one was built in 1960. It was used as a junior high gym for several years and was actually the home gym for neighboring Southwestern for two years when its gym was destroyed by a tornado in 1974.

Brown Gym is now part of the Madison Parks and Recreation Department and is used by walkers. It is also rented out for basketball, volleyball, dances and other activities.

Brown Memorial Gymnasium was dedicated in 1925. It was renovated after the flood of '37 and is now part of the Madison Parks and Recreation Department.

The Madison gym in Jefferson County is located on the banks of the Ohio River. It flooded in 1937.

Memorabilia is encased in a hallway outside the gym at Madison.

JEFFERSONVILLE

In 1937, Jeffersonville needed a fresh start. The great flood in January left destruction and ruin in its wake and kept students out of school for two months. The basketball team was unable to complete its season, playing just eleven games.

Later that year, once the Ohio River had finally receded to its banks, construction was completed on the Jeffersonville Field House (later named the Nachand Field House), and the first game was played there in January 1938. For thirty-four years, it was the popular home (sixty-five hundred fans would crowd into the building for sectional games) of the Red Devils. Too popular, it turned out.

"People would stand outside the doors, and the cops would give them the scores at the end of the quarters," said Bobby Porter, a 1954 graduate. "The fire marshal just could not let everybody in the building that wanted to be there."

Although Jeffersonville last played its games in the field house in 1971, Providence, a Catholic high school in nearby Clarksville, continued to use the facility as its home gym for several years. Indiana University–Southeast also played its home games there for a time. In 2008, the Jeffersonville girls' team played a "throwback" game in the field house against rival Silver Creek.

But the red-brown brick building with high windows is best remembered for the highly successful yet star-crossed Jeffersonville program that was twice suspended by the Indiana High School Athletic Association—in 1931 for allegedly recruiting players and for the entire season of 1949–50 for the same reason.

"Ed Denton [a 1939 Jeffersonville graduate] was coaching, then allegedly brought a couple players in from Silver Creek," said Pete Obremskey, a 1954 Indiana all-star who started two years for Branch McCracken's teams at Indiana. "The Silver Creek people reported him to the IHSAA and got Jeffersonville suspended for a year."

The Red Devils made a strong recovery, though, and under coach Bill Johnson were ranked number one most of the 1952–53 season. Standing in Jeffersonville's way in the sectional final that year was much-despised Silver Creek, the school Jeffersonville blamed for putting it on probation three years earlier.

"[The Jeffersonville Field House] was alive," Obremskey said. "Poor Bill Johnson could hardly contain himself. It was about as tense as I've ever seen a coach. The gym was just electric."

Jeffersonville won the game, 39–35, and advanced all the way to the round of sixteen, where it lost to eventual state runner-up Terre Haute Gerstmeyer. The Red Devils also won regionals in 1954 and '58—and thirteen total from 1934 to 1992—before finally winning a state title in 1993.

Left: The Jeffersonville Red Devils last used the field house as their home gym in 1971, but Providence used it for several years after.

Below, left: An exterior look at the Jeffersonville gym, built in 1937.

Below, right: The Jeffersonville (Nachand) Field House is now used by the Jeffersonville Parks and Recreation Department. It is open six days a week.

The Nachand Field House is now owned and operated by the Jeffersonville Parks and Recreation Department and hosts basketball and volleyball leagues and a number of other activities. It is open six days a week. It is also flush with memorabilia from the Red Devils' glory days.

"I broke my foot as a senior right before the tournament my senior year and had to get a special boot made," Obremskey said. "I had a chance to look around the field house one game as I was sitting there and soak in how special it was. Other than our team, there wasn't much going on in Jeffersonville. It was the social event of the week. It was the place to be."

MIDDLETOWN

Of the thirteen buildings constructed by the Work Projects Administration in Henry County in the 1930s, the Middletown gym was the biggest. Built in 1939 with Indiana stone visible both inside and out, the gym had a distinctive look.

"It wasn't fancy," said Tom Furnish, a 1941 graduate who played in the first game in the gym, a win over Knightstown. "It was huge compared to some of the county schools we played against, like Cadiz and Sulpher Springs, where they only had three rows of bleachers on each side."

The Middletown gym had ten rows of bleachers on each side, a stage on the east end and a rock wall on the west end that served as a quasi balcony, where mostly kids would watch the game. The capacity, still listed above the ticket window in the west lobby, is 1,306.

"The way that place was built, it was not going to rot and rust away," said Dallas Hunter, a starter on the 1951 sectional championships. "It was entirely built of rock, even the divisions between the dressing rooms were all stone."

The Cossacks originally played in a tiny gym in the basement of the school, located across the street to the west of the new gym. It was later turned into a room for shop class.

"[The old gym] had a six-foot wall all the way around it," Hunter said. "It was like from the move *Hoosiers* but smaller. The dressing rooms were down underneath the bleachers."

Middletown won two sectionals—in 1929 and '38—before moving to the new gym, which was massive compared to the old one. When Von Jameson, a 1932 Middletown graduate, returned to his alma mater as coach in 1947, the Cossacks really got rolling. Middletown won the New Castle Sectional five times (1951, '54, '56, '60 and '62) despite never having an enrollment of more than two hundred students.

"Mr. Jameson did things the way he wanted to do them, and the boys that played for him respected him or they didn't play," Hunter said. "There weren't tryouts. He invited the boys out he knew he wanted."

When Hunter was a sophomore, Jameson told him he didn't want just anybody to take over the program when he decided to step down. He told Hunter he'd like for it to be him. Fifteen years later, it happened.

"That's how far ahead he could see things happen," Hunter said. "He had a knack for that. There we were all those years later, in that very same gym where he told me that, and he was introducing me as the new coach. It was shocking to me."

Hunter coached Middletown in its final two years. In 1967, it was consolidated with Cadiz and Sulphur Springs to form Shenandoah. The Shenandoah School Corporation still owns the gym, and it is used for middle school games and practices. A few blocks away, in the Middletown–Fall Creek Township Historical Society, are several Middletown basketball artifacts, including a traveling jug passed around between county schools.

The gym appears as rock solid as ever and probably isn't going anywhere soon.

"It'd take an army to bring it down," Hunter said. "And there'd be an army of people out there to stop them."

Middletown won the Pendleton Invitational Tournament several times through the years.

An exterior look at the Middletown gym in Henry County. It was built in 1939 with Indiana stone.

The visible rock inside the Middletown gym was a unique feature. Kids would watch games from atop a rock wall on the west end.

WILLIAMSBURG

The Williamsburg gym was almost a second home for Jon Detweiler in recent years. He looked after the former school and gym—which came under control of a board of directors when the elementary school closed in 1983—almost as if it were his own. And it was, in many ways. When Detweiler died in April 2009, many of the stories of the Williamsburg basketball teams went with him.

"Jon was six years behind me in school," said Al Dillon, a 1956 Williamsburg graduate. "He knew all the history of it. He kept that place awful nice and did so much work to it for no salary. He put a lot of time and effort into it."

The basketball court inside the Williamsburg Community Center was renamed for Detweiler in the summer of 2009, and the Jon Detweiler Memorial Shootout, a high school summer tournament, was played in both 2009 and '10.

Two months before his death, Detweiler talked about the 1954–55 Williamsburg team, which won twenty-four consecutive games before losing 58–40 to Richmond, at Richmond, in the sectional championship.

"They were the only undefeated team in the state that year and were ranked number fourteen back when there was only one class," he said. "That was probably the highlight for Williamsburg. The gym held about 925 people back in those days, and we probably packed a few more in than that in 1955."

The gym was originally built with the school in 1923 but was extensively renovated in 1953. The east wall was knocked out, and the court, which ran north and south, was reconstructed to go east and west. The bleachers and stage were ripped out and replaced with new wood bleachers.

After several down years, coach Vernon "Bob" Warner took over in 1953 and led the Yellow Jackets to a 15-6 record. The next year, led by six-foot-six twins Linville and Leon Thomas, Williamsburg won all of its regular season games, mostly by lopsided scores.

Warner, a veteran coach with "drill sergeant" qualities, according to Leon Thomas, attempted to take advantage of the twins' appearance on one occasion. In a game at Lynn, Linville picked up four fouls in the first half. At halftime, Warner instructed Linville and Leon to trade jerseys.

"Don McBride was one of the referees," Leon said. "He was well-known around there and was a lifelong friend of Warner. We didn't play twenty seconds before he blew the whistle and told Lin and I to trade jerseys. Warner had this old black hat he wore, and he just threw it on the ground."

Williamsburg never did win a sectional. It consolidated into Northeastern with three other schools in 1967. Today, the Williamsburg Community Center is used almost every day of the week in the winter for parties, leagues, reunions and other events. Much of the community center's success can be traced back to Detweiler's effort.

"We all try to pitch in," said Frank Monroe, a 1958 graduate who now looks after the community center. "From November to April, there's always something going on. That's the way you want it to be."

An exterior look at the Williamsburg school in Wayne County. The gym was built in 1923 but was renovated in 1953.

The Williamsburg gym and school are now used as a community center. The court was named for Jon Detweiler, who spearheaded efforts to keep the gym going. The 1955 team won twenty-four games to start the season.

GASTON

For all the wins the Gaston Bulldogs posted in the 1950s, Guy "Bub" Millspaugh's best memory of his hometown gym came in a loss. It was on a cold winter night during the 1954–55 season.

"Yorktown had a really good team that won the [Delaware] county tournament that year," said Millspaugh, then a junior. "They had Muncie Central upset at the Muncie Field House but missed wide-open layup in the final seconds. Muncie Central was ranked number one most of that year [lost to eventual state champion Crispus Attucks 71–70 in the round of eight]. Our coach, Phil Hodson, was from Yorktown and came to Gaston for his first coaching job. They got way ahead of us and were up by thirteen going into the fourth quarter, but we came back in the fourth and only lost by three. My uncle only saw me play one time, and it was that game. He said it was the best high school game he'd ever seen."

There weren't many people who did see it. The place was packed, as usual, but the 1923 gym was cozy. There were six rows of permanent wood bleachers on one side, four on the other and room for a few more on the south end. On the north side was a stage, and above both entrances was a crow's-nest where a few more people could sit when it was especially crowded.

Above the gym was an auditorium, a few classrooms and a principal's office. The two-story brick schoolhouse was located east of the gym but has since been torn down.

"Our basketball teams were good in spells," said Bob Geimer, class of 1956. "We had some good years in the '50s. Guy Millspaugh could really shoot the lights out."

Gaston won the county tournament in '56 and '57 under Hodson, for the first time since the early '40s. The Bulldogs would play the county and sectional tournaments at the Muncie Field House, a more-than-six-thousand-capacity building that dwarfed the Gaston gym.

"The Muncie Field House was remarkable to us," Millspaugh said. "It's a treasure. The Gaston gym was kind of a treasure, too."

Gaston consolidated with rival Harrison Township in 1966 to form Wes-Del. The former high school gym is now used as a community center and is available to rent for $12.50 an hour. Its unusual wood exterior was done as part of a remodeling in the 1980s; it was originally grayish stucco.

In recent years, a three-point line was added to the court, which is painted blue and white and has a Bulldog in the center circle. The court is so narrow, though, that the arc only extends to barely below the free throw line.

"It wasn't made for three-pointers," Millspaugh said with a laugh. "But we had some games in there."

Opposite, top: The Gaston gym in Delaware County is now used as a community center and is available to rent. A wood exterior was added on in the 1980s.

Opposite, bottom: Gaston's gym was built in 1923. The three-point line, added in the 1980s, only extends to the free throw line before it runs out of bounds.

LADOGA

One of Indiana's classic nicknames is the "Canners" from Ladoga. The name was uniquely tied to the community, as the Ladoga Canning Company operated in town from 1903 to 1950 and employed about three hundred people at its peak. It was a particularly busy time during World War II, when the Ladoga Canning Company was a major supplier of produce shipped overseas.

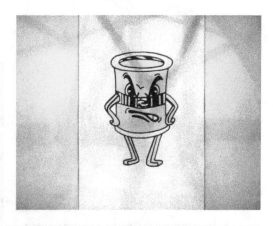

Maybe even better than the nickname, though, is the Canner mascot that graces both the wall mat and center court at the Ladoga gym, now part of an elementary school. The logo features any angry-looking can with a furrowed brow and his lip snarled to show his teeth. Protruding from the can are two skinny arms and legs; his hands are on his hips.

"I used to work at the Canning Company in the summertime," said Mort Kimmel, a 1952 Ladoga graduate. "We'd haul those tomatoes from our fields to the Canning Company. It was a major business in Ladoga."

The angry Canner mascot had no effect on Waveland's Keith Greve one night during the 1951–52 season. Greve, an Indiana Basketball Hall of Famer who played four years at Butler, outscored Ladoga's team by himself with forty-two points in a 92–41 win.

"He was an outside shooter, but he could score from anywhere," Kimmel said.

The Ladoga gym, opened in 1941 as a post-Depression Work Projects Administration construction, was one of the biggest in the twelve-school county. The gym was built with a four-foot wall surrounding the perimeter of the court, with a stage on the east end and more seating, behind an eight-foot brick wall with a railing, on the west end.

The green-and-gold Canners were originally known as the Spartans, but the name was changed in 1931 when the Canning Company bought new uniforms for the team. Ladoga had previously played in the basement of the two-story brick schoolhouse, built in 1918. Prior to that, Ladoga's teams played in a room above the town hall and on a dirt floor inside the Ladoga Christian Tabernacle.

"The saying was, 'That's where [opponents] ate our dust,'" said Bill Boone, a 1956 Ladoga graduate who has researched Ladoga and Montgomery County basketball history extensively.

Ladoga's new gym was a palace compared to some of the others in the county. The New Ross gym was basically a barn with a potbellied stove on each end.

Left: The Ladoga gym in Montgomery County was built in 1941.

Opposite, inset: The Ladoga Canners had one of the most unusual nicknames in the state. The elementary school teams have retained the name and the gym.

Below, inset: An exterior look at the Ladoga gym in Montgomery County.

"It was freezing cold playing there in the middle of the winter," Boone said. "There was no other place like that. There was sort of a heavyset guy on our team in high school, and he fell right through the floor during one game."

Ladoga played Crispus Attucks three times in the early 1950s, when the all-black Indianapolis school was starting its dynasty. The Canners lost all three games, but the 1952 game played at Crawfordsville drew such a crowd that it allowed Ladoga to buy new glass backboards.

Despite a successful run from the 1920s to the late 1950s under coaches Floyd "Doc" Neff, Jerry Steiner and Jack Hester, Ladoga never won a sectional. The 1936 team went 17-4 under Neff but lost 33–28 to Crawfordsville in the sectional championship.

Ladoga consolidated into Southmont in 1971. The gym continues to be used by the elementary school and as a gathering spot for alumni reunions every year.

GREENS FORK

There's no gym floor, no baskets—hardly a trace that it was once a basketball gym. Two fire trucks are parked on a concrete floor in what looks like nothing more than a makeshift garage. More than seven decades ago, though, this was the home of the 1935–36 Greens Fork Demons, a team that even now is revered in this Wayne County community in eastern Indiana.

"The last member of that team died [in 2009]," said Phyllis Beers, a 1954 Greens Fork graduate. "I'm not old enough to have seen them play. But I feel like I grew up loving that team because I heard so much about them."

Richmond had dominated the smaller Wayne County Schools before 1936, winning six consecutive sectionals and regional championships in '34 and '35. Led by second-year coach Al Brown, Greens Fork pummeled Webster (38–14) and Boston (32–18) to reach the championship against Richmond. It was never a game. The smaller Demons, led by sixteen points from Rex Ellis, won 34–20. A newspaper article at the time said, "Sirens blew and no one slept" in Greens Fork and called Brown "the toast of the town."

The unlikely run didn't end there, as Greens Fork defeated heavily favored Muncie (at the Muncie Field House) 25–22 in the afternoon game of the regional. New Castle finally ended the Demons' season that night in the regional championship, winning 33–20.

The spacious gymnasiums at Richmond and Muncie were a far cry from Greens Fork, where barely three hundred people could cram into the 1925 gym. The layout was unusual. There was a balcony along the west wall with a row of chair-back seats and three more rows of wood bench seats. An iron staircase led down from the balcony to floor level. The back row of theater-style seats on the floor was flush against the west wall, with each row in front of it descending into a sort of pit area. The playing floor was about three feet above the front row of seats, essentially giving the appearance of playing games on a stage.

"Fountain City and Milton had the same style," said George Turner, a 1950 graduate. "People would run right off that stage all the time."

Until 1949, there was a booth about eight feet off the floor on the east wall where two students would sit and drop wooden numbers into slots that served as the scoreboard.

"There was no clock," Turner said. "They kept it at the scorer's table, but we had no idea if there was five minutes left or twenty seconds."

Greens Fork never won another sectional after '36. The school, along with neighboring Economy, was absorbed by Hagerstown in 1963. The school was used as a junior high until 1971 and later as a manufacturing plant and a Case IH farm equipment dealer. It's been used as a fire station for more than ten years. The only remnant of Greens Fork athletics in the gym is a track and field record board, with many of the top marks from the 1940s and '50s.

Fire trucks are now parked on what was the basketball court at Greens Fork.

A board of old track records hangs in the gym/fire station in Greens Fork.

The Greens Fork gym and school, built in 1925, are now used by the local fire department.

UNION TOWNSHIP

While stationed in Rhode Island in the early 1940s, O.J. Sloop played on an army base basketball team that scrimmaged against Rhode Island State College. Rhode Island's coach was Frank Keaney, one of the originators of the fast break offense and full-court pressing defense.

Sloop struck up a friendship with Keaney—later naming his son after him—and brought many of his philosophies back with him after fighting in World War II when he was hired out of Butler at his alma mater, Union Township, in 1946.

"A lot of the things he learned there, he put to use here," said Lorene Sloop, his widow. "His ideas on the fast break came from Keaney. We had smaller teams here so we always played that style."

It suited Union Township well. The Ramblers played in a gym in rural Johnson County that was constructed in 1928 after a fire destroyed the previous school. It was a small gym, with five rows of bleachers on the north and south sides and a stage on the east end. It had a double ten-second line, like many gyms at the time.

Union Township won county tournaments in 1948 and '49, and the school's only sectional championship in '52.

"We ran teams into the ground," said Noble Spicer, who played on Sloop's first two teams at Union Township. "Our gym was small, but our floor was the same size as Franklin's. We got up and down the court. Teams had a hard time keeping up with us."

Lorene Sloop (her maiden name was Baker) graduated from Union Township in 1942. O.J. Sloop's father, Otis, also coached at Union Township, and Lorene's father, Custer Baker, coached at Center Grove from 1926 to 1929.

"I don't know how many games I've been to," Lorene said with a laugh. "I've seen most of the great players in the state because we'd go to the state tournament every year. Basketball was always a first love of mine. We'd play [basketball] in phys ed in the Union gym, but the guards couldn't shoot back then. I'd get irritated when they'd put me at guard."

The gym and school are now used as a K–5 elementary. The gym has changed very little. There are banners in the gym honoring the county and sectional championship teams, as well as a blue-and-gold sign marking the "Rambler's Pep Club."

One of Lorene Sloop's most vivid memories of the gym came near the end of her husband's coaching tenure in the late 1950s.

Above: The Union Township gym in Johnson County was built in 1928 after a fire destroyed the previous school. The Ramblers won the sectional in 1952. The banner still hangs in the gym, now used by elementary students.

Opposite, inset: An exterior look at the Union Township gym and school.

"He walked clear out to about the foul line and got his first technical," she said. "It was two referees he really liked and respected. But he was really upset. When we were at home that night he said, 'That's enough.' He was done coaching after that season."

Union Township was consolidated into Franklin in 1963.

"One thing I'll always remember is that our bench was right in front of the visiting fans," Lorene said. "There was a guy from Trafalgar that would get right behind O.J. and just heckle him all game. It didn't bother O.J., but it got the boys pretty riled up."

CRAWFORDSVILLE

It was sometime in the 1970s—the exact year escapes Paul Curtis—when legendary Lebanon coach Jim Rosenstihl sidled up next to him before a game at Crawfordsville. It was always the custom of the two coaches to talk before the junior varsity game.

On this occasion, Rosenstihl took a look as fans climbed to their seats in the Crawfordsville gym and remarked, "We used to have this in Lebanon."

Rosenstihl was referring to Lebanon's Memory Hall, where the Tigers last played in 1968. Lebanon moved into a more-than-four-thousand-capacity gym, but it lacked the personality of gyms like Memory Hall, Crawfordsville's 1940 gym, called "the Pit" by local fans. It had seats all the way around with entrances in all four corners. There was a six-foot wall at each end of the court.

"It was a horrible place to practice," said Curtis, who won 169 games from 1970 to 1982, the longest tenure of any coach in Crawfordsville history. "There was no way to set up side courts because all the seats were permanent. It made it tough to schedule practice times. But for games, there wasn't a bad seat in the house. It was set up a lot like [Purdue's] Mackey Arena."

The gym did have two smaller courts beneath it that were used for physical education classes. They often served as "warm up" courts for teams waiting to play in one of the many sectional games held in the gym. There were also stories of coach Dick Baumgartner drilling his team at halftime on the practice court.

"By today's standards it wasn't that big (2,650 capacity), but it had that Roman theater feel to it with the whole floor surrounded and everybody close to the floor," said Dick Haslam, who led Crawfordsville to the state championship game in 1958 and coached at his alma mater from 1963 to 1970. "The crowd was polite, but avid. And the band was set up on one end of the floor. It was a neat gym. We won a lot of games on talent, but I know that fan support played an important factor."

Montgomery County—Crawfordsville in particular—was the breadbasket of basketball in Indiana. Though it can't be documented for sure, it's believed that the first game played in Indiana was between Crawfordsville and Lafayette at the Crawfordsville YMCA on March 16, 1894. Crawfordsville won the first state basketball tournament in 1911. When Haslam's team made it to the state finals in '58, he had his picture taken with 1911 standout Hugh Miller in the old Crawfordsville YMCA, which has since been demolished.

"Crawfordsville has a great basketball history," Haslam said. "The game has changed a lot, even since I played, but they can never take away that the first champions were from here."

The Crawfordsville gym is now used as part of a health center.

The Athenians played at the old YMCA until 1919, when they moved to the Crawfordsville Auditorium inside the school. Games were played at Wabash College from 1929 to 1935 and then at the armory until the new gym opened on January 24, 1940.

The last sectional was played there in 1971, and the last Crawfordsville game was played in 1993. After sitting empty for several years, the gym is now part of the Athena Sport and Fitness Center.

"I'm honored they let me coach there as long as they did," Curtis said. "People were very interested. I always made it a point to go downtown Saturday morning after a game, especially if we lost, because I knew everyone would want to talk about it."

OOLITIC

Dan Bush coached at Bedford North Lawrence through Damon Bailey's remarkable run to the all-time state career scoring record and state championship in 1990. But even that unique place in time—including a record 41,046 fans packed into the Hoosier Dome for the state championship—could barely rival the fervor during Bush's playing days at Oolitic in the late 1960s.

"I absolutely loved it," said Bush, a 1968 graduate who scored 1,467 points in his career. "People in their thirties and forties now don't realize what it was like back then. Cars would be lined up along the streets, or people would walk from their houses to the games. It was the event in Oolitic."

The Bearcats played in a gym built through the Works Progress Administration in 1938. It was not a regulation-size floor but had nine rows of bleachers on each side and could seat a little more than one thousand people when temporary bleachers were added at the ends of the court. Those temporary bleachers came in handy in 1953–54 and during Bush's time in the late 1960s.

Bob Lovell, a six-foot-seven standout, led Oolitic to the school's first sectional championship as a junior in 1954. The Bearcats defeated rival Bedford 56–53 in overtime in the sectional semifinals at Bedford and then pummeled Heltonville by thirty-eight in the championship.

"We had a class reunion recently, and people were asked about their favorite highlights from high school," said Larry King, who played on the 1954 team. "Almost everybody brought up that sectional championship. That was a really good team. They packed in those portable bleachers at the ends of the court, and there was barely any room to move."

One of Bush's favorite memories of the gym was a 131–71 win over Floyd Central his senior season. The other starters that year—Larry Lamb, Dave Ables, Kevin Staley and Mike Fields—all averaged in double figures.

"They started off in a box-and-one on me, and we had a lot of other guys who score," Bush said. "We pressed a lot in those days. [Coach Bob Masterson] took that press that UCLA was using under John Wooden, and that's how we got a lot of our points. It wasn't run-and-gun but full-court pressure defense."

Oolitic again beat host Bedford, 55–49, in the 1967 sectional championship.

"That place was electric," Bush said. "Our towns were two miles apart, and they were more than twice as big as us in enrollment."

The following year, Oolitic was 23-0 after winning all of its sectional games by twenty-one points or more. But the Bearcats lost 61–59 to Holland, and future ABA and NBA player Don Buse, in the first regional game at Huntingburg.

"There are people around here in their eighties who still talk about those teams," Bush said. "We thought we could have gone further in '68."

Old State Highway 37, which once ran just east of the high school, was rerouted outside of Oolitic in 1974, the same year the school was consolidated into Bedford North Lawrence. The school and gym continued as a junior high until 1986 and is now owned by the city and available to rent.

The Oolitic gym was packed in the sectional championship seasons of 1954 and 1967. It is now owned by the city.

An outdoor look at the Oolitic gym and school in Lawrence County. It was built as a Works Progress Administration project in 1938.

The scorer's table inside the Oolitic gym.

BEDFORD

When asked about the old gymnasium at Bedford—known as "the Quarry" to locals—Clarence Brown belted out a line or two from the Four Seasons' hit "December 1963 (Oh, What a Night)."

"It was loud and rowdy and everything you'd think basketball in southern Indiana should be," said Brown, a 1973 graduate. "Every time I drive by it, I thank God that I played there and wish the children today could watch just one game there to see what it was like."

Constructed in 1924 during the first wave of large gymnasiums built just for basketball, it hosted numerous sectional and regional tournaments through the years. The listed capacity was just over four thousand, but many more crammed into the facility during tournament time. In addition to the seating below, there were several rows of seating in the balcony that encircled the gym.

Despite the large capacity, dozens of fans would be left to wait in the cold and snow during sectionals, left to wait for score updates from fans through the upstairs windows or police officers at the main entrances.

"There were seats all the way around, but I was coaching at Oolitic [sectional champions in 1967 and '68] and there wasn't a seat to be had," said Bob Masterson, who coached the last two seasons at Bedford before consolidation, from 1972 to 1974. "It was pretty wild in that gym."

The Bedford Stonecutters—named for the numerous limestone quarries near Bedford—dominated the smaller county schools through the years, winning thirty-six sectional championships from 1920 to 1974. Bedford also won twenty regional championships in that span, including the final season before the school was consolidated to Bedford North Lawrence in 1974.

Brown's family—one of the few African American families in Bedford—moved to the area from Kentucky in 1955.

"All the stuff that was going on in the South in the 1960s...I was never subjected to any of that," Brown said. "We were the enemy a lot of places we went but never once was called a name or forced to go through the back door or anything like that."

Brown said one of his favorite memories at the Quarry came in a loss to Jennings County during his senior season. Brown scored thirty-three points, but Bedford lost the game. Coming out of the locker room after the game, he was stunned to see Louisville coach Denny Crum.

Above: Sunlight shines through the large windows of the Bedford gym, now used by the junior high.

Opposite, inset: The 1924 Bedford gym was known as "the Quarry." The Stonecutters hosted many sectional and regional tournaments there through the years.

"I had no idea he was there," Brown said. "We were focused on winning the game because we never beat those guys. Looking back, it was pretty neat to think he was there to see us play."

Bedford officially moved out of the Quarry and into its new gym outside of town in January 1975. The gym still stands alone on the corner of Fifteenth and O Streets and is used by the junior high. The balcony has since been taken out, and the only seats are several rows of pullout bleachers on one side.

"I wish they could have left some of that balcony there so you could see what it used to look like," Brown said. "But the important thing is that it's still there."

ORLAND

The 1933 Orland gym is intact; it just takes a little searching to find it all. The wood floor, complete with the orange tiger painted at midcourt, is usually hidden by tables and chairs on bingo night. The dropped ceiling hides the baskets on both ends of the court, held by chains thirty feet above the floor, and on the west side of the floor, where the stage was at one time, is now a bar and restaurant for the American Legion, which has owned the building since 1976.

"The actual gym really hasn't changed whatsoever," said Howard Elliott, a 1960 graduate who still lives in Orland, located in Steuben County in the far northeast corner of the state, just a few miles from the Michigan border. "The foul lines are still there, the hardwood floor and the baskets."

The school, a two-story brick building, was built in 1908 and was torn down in the late 1970s. A hallway that connected the gym to the school remains. The original wood bleachers, just a few rows on each side, have been taken out.

Before the gym was built, the Orland Tigers played their games in a barn just south of town that still stands today.

"My mom used to talk about going there," Elliott said. "It had two wood-burning stoves under the bleachers to heat it in the winter. There was a wood railing around it, and you'd have to kind of look down on the floor to watch the games."

Bob Molter, class of 1962, said Orland was more known for its baseball teams than basketball. Orland never won a sectional before it was consolidated into Prairie Heights in 1964.

"We had some decent teams and had fun playing," Molter said. "The gym over at Salem Center [south of Orland in Stueben County], they turned into a horse barn. You'd be dribbling the ball over there and hit a flat spot, and the ball wouldn't bounce. Our gym, I don't think anybody had a floor as nice as ours. It's still in really good shape."

The gym is used for bingo, as well as gatherings for reunions and wedding receptions.

Opposite, top: An exterior shot of the Orland gym in Stueben County, built in 1933.

Opposite, bottom: Bingo games are the main use for the Orland gym these days. Above the dropped ceiling are the original baskets.

BROWNSBURG

In two years as Brownsburg's boys' coach and nineteen more with the girls, Mike Griffin coached more games than anyone at Brownsburg's Varsity Gym. After the 2000–01 season—coincidently, two years after rival and neighboring Avon built its new gym—Brownsburg moved into Varsity Field House.

"It wasn't quite the same," Griffin said. "The noise just reverberated in the Varsity Gym, unlike the new one. It reinforced to the crowd to keep doing what they were doing."

The Varsity Gym was built in 1957 and replaced the College Avenue Gym, which was a Brownsburg landmark in its own right. The College Avenue Gym was used in the movie *Hoosiers*, including the scene where assistant coach Shooter Flatch (played by Dennis Hopper) stumbled onto the court drunk in the middle of a game. *Hoosiers* director and producer Angelo Pizzo watched Hopper prepare for the scene.

"He was out in the middle of the hallway spinning himself around and around," Pizzo said. "That's what you see in the movie."

Brownsburg's teams started out playing in an upstairs assembly room at the high school. The College Avenue Gym was dedicated on January 30, 1929, in front of Indiana High School Athletic Association commissioner Arthur Trester (a 32–22 loss to Pittsboro). It had a balcony on the north end and "more electronically lighted exit signs than any institution this side of the New York subway," according to the local newspaper.

"Even if there was 150 people in there, it felt like you were playing for the national

championship," said Griffin, who coached junior high teams for eight years there.

The construction of the Varsity Gym—which featured concrete seating all the way around the floor that looked down on the action and a few rows of pullout bleachers on each side of the court—in 1957 allowed Brownsburg to host the sectional tournament. The Bulldogs capped an impressive run in the 1950s with a sectional championship in '59 under coach Lucas Cevert. Brownsburg didn't win in 1961 (Plainfield did), but it was memorable for another reason.

"Everybody got snowed in the gym one night of the sectional," said Gary Gordon, a 1964 graduate. "I lived a block away so I went home, changed clothes and came back. Everybody stayed, and they just had a dance."

Griffin's girls' team played a single game at the gym in 2002 because of a scheduling conflict. The gym was leased from the school by the Brownsburg Parks and Recreation Department from 2005 to 2009 but now sits empty. Athletic director Greg Hill said in July 2010 that "nothing will be going on in that gym in the foreseeable future."

Above: The Varsity Gym in Brownsburg was built in 1957 and replaced the 1929 College Avenue Gym that was featured in *Hoosiers*. It was used as a community center until 2009. The school owns the building, but it's unclear how it will be used in the future.

Opposite, inset: An exterior look at the Varsity Gym in Brownsburg. It hosted several sectional tournaments in Hendricks County.

SULLIVAN

It was bitterly cold and snowing when Evansville Bosse visited Sullivan in the winter of 1980–81. Girls' basketball in its current form was still in its infancy. Outside, snow fell to the ground as the temperature dipped below twenty degrees. Inside, it couldn't get much hotter.

"That was probably the most memorable game we had there," said Drew (Bock) Lisman, who guided Sullivan through a remarkable eight-year run into the mid-1980s. "I remember looking around, and it was completely packed. It was amazing. They were standing in the aisles."

It was no small feat to fill up the Sullivan gym, which listed a capacity of twenty-seven hundred when it opened in 1928. It was built with eleven rows of bleachers all the way around and entrances leading onto the court from each of the four corners. A unique feature was the 208 "opera-style" seats that encircled the court, right on top of the action.

"Everybody always wanted to get into those seats," said Jim Hartman, who coached football and was an assistant for basketball in the 1950s and '60s. "They were right there on top the action, just a few feet from the floor."

John Robbins got his first boys' basketball coaching job at Sullivan in 1964. He remembered it as "more of a football community" in his three years there, but his first team did win a sectional despite just a 6-13 record entering the tournament.

Sullivan won its dedication games at the new gym on February 23, 1928, with the girls defeating Linton 23–17 and the boys topping Carlisle 43-33. Sullivan then hosted the boys' sectional a week later (there was not a girls' tournament until the 1970s) and lost to Carlisle, the eventual champion, in the second round. It was the sectional site until 1967.

Larry Bird's Indiana State team played an intra-squad exhibition game at Sullivan, located twenty-five miles south of Terre Haute, before the national championship season of 1978–79.

"That was quite a deal," Hartman said. "We had a really nice crowd here, and they ran through a practice, then played a game. Bird was getting quite a bit of publicity by then."

Though the Sullivan boys' teams went through a dry spell of sectional championships despite some very good teams in the late 1970s, the girls picked up the slack. Maria Stockberger was Sullivan's first and only Indiana all-star in 1985 and helped the Golden Arrows to an 80-7 record in four years. The 1982 team won the semistate.

"The girls were as fun to watch as the guys and were tremendously supported,"

Left: The Sullivan gym opened in 1928 with a listed capacity of twenty-seven hundred.

Below: Sullivan hosted sectionals several times after this gym was built. The gym was bought at a public auction in May 2010 by doctor Ted Lim. There are plans to make it a community center.

Opposite, inset: An exterior look at the Sullivan gym in Sullivan County.

Lisman said. "A lot of our girls played against the guys."

The Sullivan teams moved out of downtown and into a new gym at the school in the late 1980s. The Southwest School Corporation put the gym up for public auction in May 2010, and it was purchased by local doctor Ted Lim, who plans to make it a community center.

A community center was the original idea. The dedication program from 1928 read: "The Community Gymnasium and all its activities and interests deserve the support of everyone, to the end that the greatest use may be had of it for the benefit of greatest number."

MARTINSVILLE

Prior to a middle school game several years ago at Martinsville's Glenn Curtis Gymnasium, Martinsville West Middle School assistant principal Gary Dean heard a visiting player remark, "This is the floor John Wooden played on." Dean smiled and thought, "Sort of."

An extensive renovation of the Glenn Curtis Gymnasium from 1979 to 1981 significantly altered its appearance on the interior of the gym, now adjacent to the middle school. The permanent bleachers were torn out and replaced with retractable bleachers and a running track above that circles the court. The wood floor was replaced with a Tartan surface popular in the 1970s.

Only the outside of the gym and the main entrance on the west side of the building resemble their appearance on February 21, 1924, when Shelbyville arrived for a dedication game at the new gym.

It was a historic night, in more ways than one. Martinsville's fifty-two-hundred-capacity gym seated more people than lived in the Morgan County community at the time (about forty-eight hundred). It was larger than gyms at Indiana or Purdue and the largest high school gym in Indiana at the time. In building it, Martinsville tipped off an arms race in the 1920s as similar-sized gyms popped up all over the state.

Wooden was an eighth-grader at Martinsville in February 1924 and didn't play in the dedication game.

"It was an incredible night," said Elmer Reynolds, a local historian who has researched Martinsville's basketball history extensively. "Many dignitaries from state government were there, and the gym was noted in 'Ripley's Believe it or Not,' a nationally syndicated column written by Robert Ripley. They were literally hanging from the rafters. One boy strapped himself by his belt to one of the beams that ran up to the ceiling."

Shelbyville, which had several fans turned away at the doors, won the game. But the Artesians went on to win the state championship several weeks later at the old coliseum in Indianapolis. It was the beginning of a golden era in Martinsville: with Wooden at guard, Martinsville made

The entrance of the Martinsville gym is much the same as it was when the gym was built in 1924. It is now part of Martinsville West Middle School. A photo of legendary John Wooden, a 1928 Martinsville graduate, hangs inside the west entrance. He led Martinsville to the 1927 state title.

the state championship game every year from 1926 to 1928, winning in 1927. The Artesians won another state title under Curtis in 1933.

"Most of them are gone now, but for years people here never forgot those teams," said Bette Dunn, a former cheerleader and 1949 graduate who later wrote for the local newspaper for four decades. "The guys who played on those teams were like heroes. My brother Sam was on the 1943 team that won a regional and got me hooked on basketball, like everybody else here."

Wooden once told Reynolds that the Martinsville gym "was the loudest of any place I've ever experienced in basketball." He also recalled Wooden telling him of his tradition of finding his wife, Nell, usually sitting with the pep band, before the game and giving her a wink.

Today, in the west lobby outside the gym, there are banners of several of Martinsville's former rivals, including the Seymour Owns, Jeffersonville Red Devils and Franklin Grizzly Cubs. Hanging upside down from the ceiling is the center circle, a wooden "M" cut out of the original floor. There are also large photos of Wooden and Curtis.

The Martinsville gym hosted several sectional and regional tournaments through the years, the last regional in 1962. Martinsville played its last high school games there in 1976. Nunn remembers a sign that was posted on the wall outside the west entrance with the Grantland Rice quote: "When the great scorer comes to write against your name, he writes not that you won or lost, but how you played the game."

Opposite, top inset: An exterior shot of the 1924 Martinsville gym.

Opposite, bottom inset: The interior of the Martinsville gym was extensively renovated in the late 1970s and early '80s.

KINGMAN

When the Kingman Community Church bought the former Kingman high school gym several years ago for $5,000, the cleanup job was immense.

"Pigeons had taken over the place," said pastor Bob Kruea. "We backed up the trucks and started scooping."

The Kingman gym was built in 1936, the same year the Black Aces claimed their only sectional championship in school history. The reddish brown brick gym had two entrances on the east side of the building, nine rows of bleachers on each side and a stage on the west end. The floor is worn by many years of neglect and wear from the time the school moved in 1965, but the gym looks much the same today as it did in the 1960s, with a gold "K" at center court and a forest green curtain covering the stage.

"We had our fiftieth class reunion in there [in 2006] and it was almost just like I remembered," said Dale Cates, a 1956 graduate. "After the school closed, they had roller-skating in there, so that couldn't have been good on the gym floor."

After Howard Decker (the coach who led Kingman to its lone sectional title) left in 1943, Kingman shuffled through coaches at an even faster rate than most small schools. From 1943 to 1965, Kingman went through eleven coaches, with only one (Dave Curtis, from 1959 to 1963) staying more than two years.

"We went through quite a few," said Richard Tunin, a 1952 graduate. "If they were any good, they would go somewhere bigger. That's how it was at a small school like ours."

Kingman had some good teams but could never break through and win another sectional. There were some memorable games and moments, though, particularly when the rival Tangier Tigers came to town from Parke County.

"We were playing Tangier my senior year, and we were up by two points," Cates said. "They went in for a shot and got fouled. The ball hit the net but never got above the rim. The referee called it good, then made free throw, and we lost by one point."

There was also the time a few years earlier when Kingman's Walter Nixon got mixed up and scored a basket for Tangier.

"They never let me play anymore," Nixon said with a laugh. "Everybody sure remembered that play, though."

The original school building was torn down, but the classrooms attached to the west of the gym are still used for Sunday school classes. Below the gym, once a lunch room and kitchen, is now used by the church for various programs. There are plans to give the gym floor a much-needed refurbishing, but that's a minor concern considering the run-down state of the gym when the church moved in.

"It's taken a lot of prayers and a lot of work," Kruea said.

The Kingman Community Church now uses the gym and adjoining classrooms.

The interior of the Kingman gym looks much the same as it did when the school was consolidated in 1965.

The exterior of the Kingman gym in Fountain County, built in 1936.

SHERIDAN

Sheridan was battling Lapel one winter night during the 1950–51 season, and the gym was even hotter than usual. Sheridan coach Larry Hobbs called a timeout.

"I said, 'Coach, can't we open some windows?'" recalled Tom Coppess, then a junior. "He said, 'Look up there. They are open.'"

Coppess looked up at windows, which were open but filled with faces looking down onto the court. Unable to get into the gym, which seated more than two thousand people, some fans had climbed onto the roof to watch rather than go home.

"I'll never forget that scene," Coppess said. "There were people everywhere. They were in the windows, seated on the floor in front of the bleachers, sitting on the stage. Wherever they could find a place. We won the game—like we usually did in that gym."

Hobbs was at the helm for a glorious era at Sheridan. The Blackhawks won seven consecutive sectionals from 1949 to 1955, including regional titles in 1950 and '55. In twenty-five seasons overall as a coach, including stops at Scircleville, Kempton, Forest and Rossville, Hobbs had just three losing seasons.

"We hosted the sectional, but Hobbs got to winning so much that they made us split the sectional with Noblesville and Tipton," said Rex Pitts, a 1952 graduate. "We had such a home court advantage, I can't really argue with that logic. One of

the sportswriters wrote at the time that if they picked up the floorboards at the Sheridan gym and moved them to Butler Field House, Sheridan would win the state tournament."

Until 1931, Sheridan played its games on the second floor of a downtown building. The new gym was constructed inside of the high school building and was one of the nicest of its era. Fans entering the gym would walk down to their seats, with several rows of permanent wood bleachers on the north and south sides and the west end. A stage with more available seating was on the east end.

Sheridan played its varsity games there until 1979. One of the unique features of the gym was a small cutout area near the court on the west end for concessions.

Until 2010, when a new school was built, it was Adams Elementary. Rocky Shanehsaz purchased it in November 2009 for $85,000. He plans to turn the school into the Hamilton County Convention Center.

In July 2010, former Sheridan students said goodbye to the school—and gym in particular—at an all-class reunion.

"It looked better than ever," Pitts said. "It was a great feeling back in our time to walk into that gym and know it would be packed every night. For that time in the 1950s, it was the mecca. People would come from other towns to see a game in the Sheridan gym."

The 1931 gym at Sheridan was built inside the school. It hosted several sectional tournaments through the years.

The Sheridan Blackhawks in Hamilton County won the sectional every year from 1949 to 1955, including regionals in '50 and '55.

An exterior look at the Sheridan gym. It was used as Adams Elementary until 2010. There are plans to convert it into the Hamilton County Convention Center.

ALPHABETICAL LIST OF GYMS

Michigan City Elston	164	Vallonia	40
Middletown	180	Vernon	48
Milroy	28	Versailles	174
Mitchell	146	Vincennes Lincoln	86
Monroe City	78	Warren	88
Moores Hill	136	Washington	84
Mooresville	102	Waveland	36
Morocco	112	West College Corner	152
Mt. Olympus	114	Wheatland	76
Mt. St. Francis	160	Williamsburg	182
New Castle	156	Winslow	94
Newport	52		
Oolitic	194		
Orland	198		
Otwell	96		
Owensville	90		
Paris Crossing	44		
Pennville	68		
Perry Central	22		
Peru	12		
Pierceton	168		
Pine Village	74		
Pleasantville	66		
Roll	24		
Royal Center	118		
Sandusky	16		
Sharpsville	18		
Shelbyville	62		
Sheridan	208		
Sidney	166		
Springville	134		
Stendal	122		
Stilesville	38		
Stinesville	132		
Sullivan	202		
Union Mills	158		
Union Township	190		

ABOUT THE AUTHOR

Kyle Neddenriep is a sports reporter for the *Indy Star*, where he produced the immensely popular online package of Indiana gyms on which this book is based.

Visit us at
www.historypress.net

Printed in the USA
CPSIA information can be obtained
at www.ICGtesting.com
LVHW080156161023
761159LV00058B/36

9 781540 224200